The Captive Superpower

How Lobbying Subverted America's Foreign Policy

Hichem Karoui

Global East-West (London)

Copyright © 2025 by Hichem Karoui

Collection: History Fo All.

Global East-West (London).

All rights reserved.

No portion of this book may be reproduced in any form without written permission from the publisher or author, except as permitted by copyright law.

Contents

1. The Foundations of American Democracy   1
   Economics and the Birth of a Nation

2. The United States in the Two World Wars   17
   Symbols of Democracy and Freedom

3. The Post-War order and the Promise of the United Nations   33
   American Leadership in World Peace

4. The Birth of Israel and the Truman Doctrine   51
   A Colonial Fact

5. Cold War Calculations   69
   Israel, a Destabilising Factor for Stabilising the Region

6. The Creation of AIPAC and Modern Zionist Lobbying   87
   Organisation, Money and Influence

7. From Capitol Hill to the White House   103
   How Lobbying Has Reshaped American Politics

8. Silencing Debate 119
   Media Narratives and the Cost of Dissent in Washington

9. Occupation and Colonial Expansion 137
   American Coverage of Israeli Wars and Colonisation Projects

10. The Erosion of American Credibility 153
    The Global Perception of Hypocrisy

11. The Dream of a Greater Israel and the Role of the United States 167
    Netanyahu's Vision and Washington's Policy

12. The America that Fought Fascism No Longer Exists 185
    Anti-Popular Wars in the Service of Big Business

Recommended Reading 203

1
The Foundations of American Democracy
Economics and the Birth of a Nation

The Influence of Wealth on the Founding Fathers

The economic backgrounds of the key figures in American history had a profound impact on the nation's creation and the formation of its political structure. The Founding Fathers — notably George Washington, Thomas Jefferson, and Alexander Hamilton — were shaped by their economic circumstances, which significantly influenced their perspectives on governance, finance, and power. Washington, for example, was a wealthy landowner and businessman who used his financial resources and social connections to exert influence and navigate the political landscape during the Revolution and the early years of the republic. His economic situation enabled him to finance military campaigns, mobilise support for independence, and ultimately secure a leading role in founding the nation.

Similarly, Jefferson's position as a wealthy plantation owner in Virginia afforded him considerable wealth. It allowed him to become familiar with the intricacies of the agrarian economy and the interests of the southern states. This background profoundly influenced his advocacy of states' rights and agricultural policies within the newly formed government.

In contrast, Alexander Hamilton was born out of wedlock and raised in poverty in the Caribbean, which provided him with a distinctly different economic background from many of his contemporaries. His experiences of poverty, coupled with his keen understanding of commerce and finance, shaped his vision of a robust national economy and a strong central government. These divergent economic backgrounds led to heated debates and negotiations at the constitutional conventions over the distribution of power, representation, taxation and the establishment of a national banking system. The tensions resulting from these differing economic interests and regional disparities are evident in the drafting of the American Constitution, which required compromises and concessions to accommodate the various economic priorities and concerns of the fledgling nation. The complex interplay between money, economic philosophies and geopolitical interests played a central role in establishing the foundations of the American political and economic landscape, creating a legacy that continues to resonate in contemporary policymaking and governance.

Constitutional Conventions and Monetary Interests: Balancing Power and Financial Interests

As the nation's founding document, the Constitution was not immune to the influence of wealth and economic interests. The delegates who gathered to draft the Constitution in 1787 had personal financial motivations that inevitably shaped the framework of the nascent republic. Recognising the potential conflict between the states and the central government over economic matters, the framers spent a long time deliberating over how economic power should be divided between the federal and state levels. This interplay of economic imperatives was central to their discussions, as balancing commercial influences with democratic governance was of the utmost importance. Financial interests influenced debates over fiscal powers, monetary regulation and trade treaties, and the resulting compromises determined the United States' economic trajectory.

Furthermore, this fundamental conflict defined the nature of federalism and influenced the development of the American political economy for centuries to come. To grasp the true levers of power that have shaped the nation's trajectory, it is essential to understand the subtle and often hidden intersections between money and politics. This chapter is based on an uncompromising exploration of the hidden alliances between economic elites and government authorities that continue to exert a profound, albeit discreet, influence on contemporary policymaking and domestic affairs.

Federalism Unveiled: The Economic Impulse in State Power versus National Power

The concept of federalism has been intimately linked to American governance since the nation's inception, shaping the distribution of power and resources between the states and the federal government. Analysing the economic foundations of federalism reveals that monetary forces and special interests heavily influence the interaction between state and national government prerogatives. Ultimately, the tug-of-war between state sovereignty and federal authority is often catalysed by economic agendas.

Throughout history, states have defended their autonomy in developing economic policies that meet regional needs, which are sometimes at odds with national strategies. This tension reflects the constant tug-of-war between economic actors vying for advantageous positions in the overall political landscape. Due to their significant financial interests, industries and businesses often try to influence state and federal allegiances through lobbying and influence peddling, thereby shaping economic policies that favour their specific enterprises. Geopolitical interests further embellish this complex dance of power.

Key industries, strategically located across the country, influence resource allocation and the formulation of trade policy. This forces state and federal authorities to engage in delicate negotiations to protect their constituents' interests. This constellation of economic motivations invariably shapes federal-state dynamics, manifesting as a labyrinth of regulations and incentives that dictate the flow of capital and resources. Consequently, the economic momentum of the struggle between state and national power is a poignant emblem of the multifaceted interaction between money, politics and geopolitics. This embodies a perpetual struggle for influence and control, where economic titans and geopolitical strategists intertwine their ambitions within the fabric of federalism. Understanding this intricate relationship is crucial for grasping the profound eclecticism that characterises modern American governance, where economic imperatives are deeply interwoven with the institutional framework of federalism.

The Industrial Revolution: Mechanising Democracy, Profiting from Power

This era marks a pivotal point in American history, characterised by unprecedented economic transformation and the rise of industrial giants. As the nation transitioned from an agrarian to an industrial economy, the dynamics of power and wealth underwent radical upheaval. The shift from craftsmanship to mechanised factories reshaped the economic landscape, consolidating power and capital in the hands of a select few individuals and companies. This consolidation of power translated into considerable political influence, with industrial magnates effectively shaping policies to align with their economic interests. The monopolistic practices of these industrialists, often referred to as 'robber barons', not only allowed them to control markets but also to exert profound influence over political institutions.

While they were patrons of the arts and philanthropists, they were also ruthless businessmen who skilfully manipulated laws and regulations to ensure their economic dominance. Political debates over key economic policies such as tariffs, labour laws, and antitrust measures revealed the pervasive influence wielded by these magnates. Furthermore, the strategic alliances formed between these industrial giants and political leaders emphasised the close relationship between economic power and policymaking. The Industrial Revolution era exposed the intricate connections between corporate influence, economic policy and geopolitical interests, shedding light on the hidden motivations behind governance and legislation.

The challenges posed by rapid industrialisation prompted the government to strive for a balance between economic growth and fair representation of the growing working class. The resulting power struggles and negotiations between industrialists, labour movements, and government bodies cast a shadow over the democratic ideal, revealing the complex interplay between economic forces, political action, and social welfare. Thus, the Industrial Revolution bears witness to the lasting impact of economic power on democratic governance, emphasising the need for vigilance in preserving the integrity and inclusiveness of the political process amid relentless economic change.

Railways and robber barons: shaping politics through capital expansion

At the end of the 19th century, the expansion of railways across America played a central role in policymaking and political life. As industrialisation increased and new markets emerged, the railway industry gained considerable economic and political influence. The consolidation of railway companies under the control of powerful magnates, often referred to as 'robber barons', exemplified the height of capitalist power. Influential figures such as Cornelius Vanderbilt, Jay Gould and Leland Stanford manipulated government policy to serve their interests, creating a symbiotic relationship between business and politics. Through the strategic financing of political campaigns and the employment of lobbyists, railroad magnates secured lucrative contracts, land grants and favourable regulations that enriched their empires. This era witnessed the emergence of crony capitalism, where economic elites dictated national agendas and legislative priorities. The intertwining of corporate power and governance catalysed profound changes in the distribution of wealth and economic opportunity, perpetuating inequalities and consolidating the influence of the wealthy elite.

Furthermore, as railways expanded their networks, they impacted geopolitical strategies and territorial ambitions. The transcontinental railway, for instance, facilitated trade and enabled the United States to assert control over vast territories, thereby consolidating its influence and resources. This fusion of economic enterprise and geopolitical manoeuvring illustrates the close link between monetary interests and the expansion of American power. The interaction between railway expansion and policymaking highlights the complex relationship between wealth and influence in shaping the nation's trajectory.

By reshaping landscapes and livelihoods, these economic forces also reshaped the political landscape, redefining the boundaries of power and privilege. At the intersection of money, politics, and power, the impact of industrial expansion on democracy became increasingly apparent, reflecting how economic imperatives can influence government actions. Consequently, the legacy of the railroad barons and their enduring political influence resonates throughout history, serving as a poignant reminder of the complex relationships between wealth, politics, and national destiny.

The Rise of the War Economy: Geopolitical Strategies and Dollar Diplomacy

Following the Second Industrial Revolution, the war economy emerged in the United States, where economic and geopolitical interests converged to determine political priorities. At the heart of this transition was the demonstrated relationship between national economic power and military power. Understanding how financial and industrial forces influenced political decisions during this period is essential. Geopolitical strategies prompted the United States to reconsider its position in the global arena. Economic competition with rising powers in Europe and Asia compelled American policymakers to resort to dollar diplomacy — leveraging economic capacity to secure political influence. This approach relied on seeking out strategic resources and markets, as well as leveraging the cultural and ideological influence of American capitalism. However, the close relationship between industry and government also raised concerns about the concentration of wealth and power. Ties between big business and political leaders gradually grew closer, strengthening corporate influence over the formulation of foreign and domestic policy.

Consequently, questions arose about who the real architects of national strategy were: elected officials or influential tycoons. Furthermore, the growth of the war economy fostered a climate of confinement and expansion, with military-industrial complexes expanding in response to geopolitical entanglements. The interplay between arms production, defence spending, and international relations became inextricably linked, compelling the government to strike a delicate balance between preparedness and provocation. As the nation oscillated between isolationist sentiments and interventionist impulses, the role of wealthy elites in shaping policy decisions was scrutinised.

Amid these changes, economic factors dictated not only military capabilities, but also diplomatic manoeuvres. Manipulating financial aid, loans, and trade agreements became a means of consolidating alliances and maintaining global supremacy. However, the convergence of economic agendas and international politics raised ethical questions, sparking debates about the moral implications of using economic power as a tool of foreign policy. Exploring the rise of the war economy reveals the profound impact of the intrinsic link between money, economics, and geopolitics on the trajectory of American democracy. As we delve deeper into this complex web of historical forces, it becomes essential to untangle the layers of influence that continue to resonate in contemporary governance and world affairs.

The Dilemmas of the New Deal: Balancing Social Welfare and Commercial Interests

The Great Depression plunged the American economy into chaos, leaving one in four workers unemployed and countless families destitute. Faced with this dire situation, President Franklin D. Roosevelt introduced the New Deal: a series of programmes and reforms aimed at reviving the economy and alleviating the population's suffering. However, beneath the veneer of altruism lay a complex web of economic and political considerations that highlighted the delicate balance between social welfare and commercial interests. Powerful business magnates wielded considerable influence over policymaking, seeking to maintain their profitability despite the turmoil. At the same time, Roosevelt recognised the urgent need to intervene to prevent further social unrest and economic collapse. This led to the implementation of various policies, including the creation of public works projects, financial reforms, and the establishment of the Social Security Act.

Nevertheless, these measures were met with fierce opposition from established business interests who saw them as infringing on their autonomy and profitability. The ensuing struggle between government intervention and corporate resistance highlighted the inherent tension between social welfare and economic influence in policymaking. Geopolitical considerations also played a role in this dilemma, as the New Deal sought to strengthen the United States' position amid global economic instability. Policymakers had to strike a delicate balance between addressing humanitarian concerns and appeasing powerful commercial entities to avoid stifling economic growth. This era marked a crucial turning point in American history, with the conflict between social and commercial interests highlighting the profound influence of money and economic imperatives on policymaking. The interaction between economic forces and government intervention during the New Deal era clearly offers valuable insights into the enduring power dynamics that continue to shape political decisions today.

Lobbyists on Capitol Hill: Negotiating Political Favours

The complex network of influence that lobbyists establish in the corridors of power reflects both the democratic right to petition the government and the financial motivations behind political decisions. As economic and geopolitical interests continually clash with public policy, lobbyists act as intermediaries between businesses, interest groups and legislators. They leverage financial resources and strategic relationships to advocate for favourable legislation. The lure of financial support and political backing has long been an integral part of the American political landscape, prompting elected officials to carefully consider the demands and requests made by these interested parties. Lobbyists exert considerable influence over policy development, using economic incentives and persuasive arguments to advance their clients' objectives. The tension between protecting the public interest and appeasing political campaign donors creates a delicate balancing act for legislators, raising crucial questions about accountability, transparency, and ethical governance.

Furthermore, the influx of money into political campaigns and lobbying has exacerbated concerns about the distortion of democratic decision-making, as representatives may be influenced more by the considerable financial resources of special interest groups than by their constituents' actual needs and concerns. Understanding the symbiotic relationship between wealthy influencers and legislative action is crucial to comprehending the intricate web of power dynamics that governs modern politics. Consequently, analysing the mechanisms used by lobbyists to advocate for specific policy outcomes provides valuable insights into the multifaceted interaction between economic imperatives, geopolitical considerations and the formulation of government regulations. Dissecting the strategies and tactics employed by lobbyists on Capitol Hill uncovers the intricate patterns of influence shaping political discourse and decision-making, highlighting the ongoing negotiations between financial incentives and public interest objectives.

Campaign Finance and Electoral Strategy: Are Democracies Up for Auction?

The interaction between campaign finance and electoral strategy is a crucial aspect of modern democracies that transcends national borders to become an increasingly widespread global phenomenon. At the heart of this intersection lies the link between economic power and political action, with implications that extend far beyond the national sphere. The financial convergence with democratic processes has created an environment in which it seems as though public policymaking is up for auction to the highest bidder. The commodification of influence challenges the fundamental principles of democracy, resulting in profound inequality in civic representation.

Through this lens, we are confronted with the harsh reality that financial contributions to political campaigns exert a disproportionate influence on policy decisions, often prioritising the interests of wealthy benefactors over the real needs and aspirations of the population. Furthermore, the symbiotic relationship between capital flows and electoral outcomes amplifies the voices of corporations and special interest groups, giving them outsized influence that overshadows the collective will of ordinary citizens. The resulting landscape resembles a battlefield where financial war chests besiege the sanctity of democratic choice, eroding the very essence of representative decision-making. Beyond the national sphere, the repercussions are felt on a global scale, with geopolitical shifts and economic imperatives combining to shape the contours of international relations. Cross-border capital flows draw nations into a complex dance of strategic alignments and alliances, exerting a preponderant influence on foreign policies and diplomatic agendas. In unravelling the intricacies of electoral strategy, we must acknowledge that the democratic process is caught in a web of intersecting economic and geopolitical interests that collide with ethical boundaries and moral imperatives. Therefore, as guardians of political insight, we must be committed to exposing the mechanisms by which democracies teeter on the brink of commercialisation. By unravelling the threads that bind the economics of influence to the fabric of governance, we can rekindle enthusiasm for democratic renewal and foster systems that are resistant to the grip of monetary domination.

Globalisation and geopolitics: policymaking in the age of capital flows

The era of globalisation has redefined the dynamics of international relations, marking a significant shift in the way nations interact with one another. At the heart of this transformation lies an unprecedented flow of capital across borders, fuelled by economic integration and technological advances. It is crucial to understand the intricate relationship between capital movements and policymaking at national and international levels.

The fundamental principle underlying the influence of capital flows on policymaking is economic interdependence between nations. The shift towards a global economy has necessitated a re-evaluation of traditional notions of sovereignty, since economic decisions made in one part of the world can have repercussions across all continents. In this context, money's power transcends simple fiscal transactions, becoming a tool of influence and leverage that shapes diplomatic and political outcomes. Economic and geopolitical interests become intertwined as nations strive to remain competitive, secure access to resources and navigate the complexities of international trade. Furthermore, the influx of foreign investment and capital can significantly impact domestic policies, often prompting governments to align their agendas with the expectations of influential economic actors.

This convergence of economic and political interests highlights the complex network of relationships that underpins modern policymaking. Therefore, to understand the underlying motivations behind political decisions and international alliances, it is essential to grasp the nuances of globalisation and the associated capital flows. However, the transformative effects of global capital flows are not without controversy, as they often highlight disparities in economic power and the distribution of resources. The asymmetrical nature of global economic integration raises concerns about the potential exploitation of smaller or less developed economies by dominant global actors. Moreover, the interplay of geopolitical interests in the context of capital flows has sparked debates about the ethics and fairness of international policies, underscoring the necessity of a nuanced understanding of the intricate relationships between money, power, and politics. In conclusion, the era of capital flows and globalisation has reshaped the geopolitical landscape and the formulation of policies, emphasising the profound impact of economic interdependence on domestic and international affairs. It is crucial to analyse the intricate connections between money, power, and politics, acknowledging the wide-reaching ramifications of global capital flows on the socio-political fabric of the contemporary world.

2
The United States in the Two World Wars
Symbols of Democracy and Freedom

Economic Catalysts: Wartime Industry and Financial Mobilisation

The economic foundations of the United States' involvement in both world wars were crucial. The transformation of industries to meet substantial military requirements was a response not only to urgent wartime demands but also to deeply rooted economic and geopolitical interests.

Clearly, money played a central role in shaping US foreign policy during these monumental periods of global conflict. The pursuit of economic growth and stability, coupled with strategic geopolitical considerations, compelled the United States to play an active role in both World War I and World War II.

Economic imperatives and political decisions drove the shift from civilian to military production. This change stimulated domestic employment and economic activity. It allowed the United States to establish itself as the 'arsenal of democracy', a power capable of supplying its own forces and those of its allies. Mobilising financial resources to fund this rapid industrial expansion and arms production emphasised the interdependence of economic and military power.

Furthermore, the economic catalysts that motivated US involvement in the wars extended beyond national considerations. Geopolitical factors and the pursuit of strategic advantage on the world stage also influenced decision-making processes. The desire to shape the post-war international order and secure economic influence further emphasised the extent to which economic considerations informed this policy. This intertwining of economic and geopolitical interests paved the way for the United States' continued dominant role in world affairs in the decades to come. It is clear, therefore, that economic imperatives and geopolitical calculations were closely linked to the United States' involvement in both world wars, shaping not only the outcome of the conflicts themselves but also the subsequent trajectory of international relations.

The arsenal of democracy: American manufacturing and the war effort

When the United States entered World War II, the country's industrial might became integral to the war effort. American manufacturing was mobilised on an unprecedented scale, with factories re-equipping to produce vast quantities of military equipment, machinery, and supplies. This industry might have demonstrated the United States' economic strength and contributed significantly to the war's outcome. The increase in production was a manifestation of the power derived from economic resources. It showcased a nation's capacity to transform economic prowess into robust military capabilities, thereby shaping the geopolitical landscape. The impressive volume of weapons, vehicles and other materials produced by American factories was vital in supporting the war efforts of the US military and its allies.

Furthermore, the shift to a war economy brought economic prosperity to the United States, lifting the country out of the Great Depression. The influx of jobs and demand for goods revitalised the country's economy, demonstrating the interplay between economic interests and war policies. This symbiotic relationship between government policies and industry emphasises the profound impact of economic considerations on the course of history. Decisions regarding wartime production and resource allocation were not immune to political influence. Corporate interests, lobbying efforts and strategic alliances played a significant role in determining production priorities.

The intertwining of economic imperatives and geopolitical objectives emphasised the complexity of policymaking in times of conflict. This further highlights the merging of economic and national security interests within the broader framework of foreign policy. From a political science perspective, the concept of the 'arsenal of democracy' encompasses not only physical production, but also the leverage and influence derived from economic power. It illustrates how economic power can be used to strengthen military capabilities and secure strategic objectives on a global scale. Recognising this symbiosis sheds light on the underlying motivations and interactions of the economic forces that drive policymaking in times of war and that fundamentally shape the trajectory of international relations.

Lend-Lease and economic leverage: aid as a tool of influence

When examining the complex dynamics of international relations during times of conflict, Lend-Lease emerges as an essential instrument in shaping the global power structure. Rooted in economic pragmatism and geopolitical strategy, Lend-Lease enabled the United States to provide vital military aid to allied nations without immediate compensation, thereby laying the groundwork for future alliances and influence. The motivation behind Lend-Lease was not purely altruistic, but instead reflected the pragmatic recognition that strengthening key allies through financial and material support would ultimately serve American interests. This marked a significant evolution in American foreign policy, shifting from traditional isolationism to active involvement in foreign affairs.

Beyond its impact on the war effort, Lend-Lease also established the United States as a dominant force in post-war economic and geopolitical reconstruction, strengthening its position on the world stage. This strategic decision significantly enhanced the United States' influence on the emerging new world order, establishing a period of dominance in international diplomacy and decision-making that lasted several decades. The nuances of economic influence and the use of aid as a tool of influence reveal the merging of political and economic agendas in international relations, highlighting the interdependence of financial resources, military capabilities and geopolitical manoeuvring. Unravelling the multiple facets of Lend-Lease reveals that wartime resource allocation transcends simple benevolence. Instead, it represents the calculated deployment of economic power to shape global politics and secure long-term national interests.

War bonds and public investment: financing the fight

In times of war, the financial burden on a nation is substantial, necessitating a robust financing mechanism to support military operations. The issuance of war bonds was a crucial tool for raising the capital necessary to finance the war effort. These bonds allowed the government to mobilise public funds by appealing to patriotism and national duty, presenting investment in war bonds as an act of solidarity with the troops and in defence of the nation as a whole. This strategy provided essential financial resources and boosted public morale and unity. The sale of war bonds also helped to control inflation by reducing the excess liquidity resulting from increased government spending. Furthermore, war bonds symbolised a commitment to victory, instilling confidence and determination in citizens and soldiers alike.

Geopolitically, the issuance of war bonds demonstrated the United States' strength and determination to its allies and adversaries, shaping their perceptions of the nation's resolve in the face of conflict. The successful financing of the war through public investment strengthened the nation's position on the world stage, linking economic interests closely to geopolitical strategy. Furthermore, this process strengthened the relationship between the government and the civilian population, fostering a sense of shared sacrifice and national purpose.

Investing in war bonds also promoted long-term economic stability by channelling savings into productive uses, thereby laying the groundwork for post-war recovery and reconstruction. Ultimately, financing the war effort through war bonds underscored the complex interplay between economic imperatives and geopolitical considerations, highlighting the multifaceted nature of policymaking during pivotal historical moments.

Geopolitical Strategy: The Balance of Power in Global Conflicts

The balance of power in global conflicts during wartime is closely linked to economic and geopolitical interests. It is important to analyse how nations position themselves strategically to gain advantages and leverage their economic power. A nation's economic strength plays a crucial role in financing its war efforts and exerting influence on the global stage. During periods of significant conflict, such as World War II, economic power translates into military capabilities, ultimately shaping the geopolitical landscape. The ability to finance and sustain large-scale military operations became a determining factor in the outcome of global conflicts. In response to the challenges posed by totalitarian regimes, economic alliances between democracies emerged. These alliances were motivated by shared values and the recognition that economic and military resources needed to be consolidated and leveraged.

The intertwining of economic considerations and geopolitical strategies led to complex networks of support and cooperation among allied nations. Achieving a balance of power in a context of global conflict required astute diplomatic manoeuvring, complex economic negotiations, and clear-sighted geopolitical calculations. The question was not just one of military power on the battlefield, but also of leveraging economic power to achieve favourable outcomes. The alliances forged during this period were as much economic as defensive. Geopolitical strategy required an in-depth understanding of the economic factors that influenced nations and how these could be exploited to influence the course of history. Furthermore, navigating the delicate balance of economic and geopolitical interests demanded an acute understanding of the interplay between finance, commerce and military tactics. In essence, the world wars were a complex symphony of financial, economic, and geopolitical orchestration, in which the fates of nations were closely intertwined with the intricate interplay of money, power, and strategic objectives.

Allied oppositions: aligning with democracies against totalitarianism

The United States' alignment with other democracies in response to the rise of totalitarian regimes had a significant influence on world politics and redefined diplomatic alliances. To understand the underlying reasons behind political decisions and their implications, it is necessary to analyse this historical period through the prism of economic and geopolitical interests.

The emergence of the Axis powers, notably Nazi Germany and the Japanese Empire, posed a direct threat to democratic values and international stability. In response, the United States sought to forge alliances with other democratic nations in order to unite against the common enemy of totalitarianism. Economically, this alignment was driven by the recognition that maintaining a balance of power was crucial for ensuring international market stability. The economic interests of the United States and its democratic allies were closely linked as they sought to preserve a trading environment conducive to their prosperity.

Geopolitically, the strategic necessity of countering the Axis powers' expansionist ambitions further catalysed the alignment of democracies. Securing the support of like-minded nations became essential for the United States if it was to contain the aggressive expansion of totalitarian regimes effectively. The policies implemented during this period highlight the interdependence between economic interests and geopolitical strategy. Notably, Lend-Lease agreements symbolised the merging of economic and military resources to support allied democracies. This vital initiative provided crucial aid to countries such as the United Kingdom and China, enabling them to resist the advance of totalitarian forces. Furthermore, the formation of diplomatic and military alliances, exemplified by the Atlantic Charter and the subsequent establishment of the United Nations, demonstrated a coordinated effort to unite democratic nations based on shared economic and security interests. This profound alignment had a lasting impact on international institutions and alliances, shaping them in a manner that reflected the enduring influence of economic and geopolitical imperatives.

The lasting ramifications of this period in history should be recognised, highlighting the complex interplay between economic power and geopolitical alliances. The democracies' alignment against totalitarianism poignantly illustrates how economic and strategic considerations intersect to shape the course of world affairs, leaving an indelible mark on the fabric of international relations.

From isolation to engagement: the evolution of public opinion and policy

The shift from isolationism to active involvement in world affairs during the world wars marked a turning point not only for the United States but also for modern international relations. While American public opinion was initially opposed to intervening in European conflicts, geopolitical realities and economic interests gradually shifted the country towards a more proactive stance. The power of money and economic motivations played a decisive role in this change. As war ravaged Europe and Asia, American industries found unprecedented opportunities for expansion and profit. The war effort offered a chance for economic revitalisation, job creation, and technological progress. Recognising the economic potential of military production and arms sales to Allied nations, influential figures in industry and finance began to advocate abandoning isolationism. This view gained traction because it aligned with broader national interests, including the preservation of economic stability and the securing of markets for American exports.

Additionally, the necessity of safeguarding foreign investments and ensuring access to essential resources prompted policymakers to reconsider the United States' isolationist stance. The influence of financial elites and corporate interests was significant in shifting the country towards greater international involvement. As economic stakes grew, lobbying efforts and political contributions from powerful industrial and financial entities intensified, pushing the government to pursue policies that aligned with their interests. This transition was fuelled by the realisation that a new world order was emerging, in which economic and geopolitical dominance would be determined by active participation and influence on the world stage.

Geopolitical considerations also played a significant role in shaping public opinion and policy. The rise of totalitarian regimes threatened the balance of power and directly challenged democratic ideals and strategic interests. Concerns about the spread of authoritarian ideologies and their potential impact on international trade and security prompted a re-evaluation of American foreign policy. Aligning with like-minded democratic nations against the growing threat of totalitarianism became imperative in order to preserve shared values and maintain regional stability. Furthermore, the realisation that American prosperity was closely linked to global developments fostered a sense of interdependence and interconnectedness, prompting a re-examination of the nation's traditional aversion to foreign involvement. In conclusion, the transition from isolation to engagement was shaped by a complex network of economic incentives, internal pressures and strategic imperatives. Understanding this transformation is crucial to comprehending the enduring impact of economic and geopolitical factors on public opinion and policy in international relations.

Post-war economic planning: establishing a new world order

In the aftermath of World War II, there was a need for a fundamental reassessment of global economic and political systems. World leaders were faced with the monumental task of rebuilding a world marked by destruction and upheaval. Central to this endeavour was the need to establish a new world order that would prevent future conflicts and promote stability and prosperity. The subsequent post-war economic planning was closely linked to the exercise of power, with nations seeking to position themselves strategically and assert their influence on the international stage.

The United States, with its significant economic power and geopolitical interests, played a central role in shaping the contours of the emerging new world order and was at the forefront of this planning. A key turning point in this process was the 1944 Bretton Woods Conference, where key agreements were concluded to reshape the international monetary system. Led by influential figures such as John Maynard Keynes and Harry Dexter White, the conference established institutions such as the International Monetary Fund (IMF) and the World Bank. These were designed to promote economic cooperation and development while serving the interests of the Western powers.

The Bretton Woods system, centred on the US dollar, consolidated US dominance in global finance and trade, establishing a post-war economic structure that reflected and reinforced American hegemony. Beyond the immediate economic implications, the establishment of this new order was closely linked to geopolitical manoeuvring and the pursuit of national interests. The United States envisaged a system that would open up markets and guarantee access to vital resources, thereby consolidating its position at the heart of the global economy. This convergence of economic and geopolitical objectives underscores the crucial role of money and financial mechanisms in achieving strategic objectives and exerting influence. The choices made during this critical period had far-reaching repercussions in terms of both the dynamics of international relations and the distribution of power. Examining the post-war economic planning that led to the establishment of a new world order necessitates an understanding of the interplay between economic imperatives and geopolitical ambitions, thereby shedding light on the complex foundations of global policymaking.

The Bretton Woods System: Rebuilding the Global Economy

The post-war period offered an unprecedented opportunity to restructure the global economy. At the Bretton Woods Conference in 1944, the groundwork was laid for the establishment of an international monetary system designed to prevent the economic disasters that had devastated the world during the interwar period. Led by the United States and the United Kingdom, the conference established new institutions, including the International Monetary Fund (IMF) and the International Bank for Reconstruction and Development (IBRD), which would later become known as the World Bank. The importance of the Bretton Woods Agreement cannot be overstated. It marked a turning point in the evolution of post-war international relations and the consolidation of American economic leadership.

This system was based on the convertibility of the US dollar into gold at a fixed rate, ensuring the stability and predictability of international trade and finance. The dollar's dominant position as the global reserve currency strengthened the United States' economic influence and geopolitical standing, fostering a deep interconnection between American policy and the global financial architecture. Beyond its economic implications, the Bretton Woods system also served as a tool for advancing American policy priorities. By exerting considerable influence within the newly created institutions, the United States was able to promote its agenda strategically and shape the economic policies of other nations. This power dynamic highlighted the intersection between economics and geopolitics, emphasising how monetary mechanisms were employed to achieve broader strategic goals.

However, the Bretton Woods system faced challenges as the post-war period progressed. Economic disparities, monetary imbalances and pressure from American commitments abroad put the stability of the established framework under strain. Ultimately, these pressures led to the system's collapse in the early 1970s, marking a significant shift in the global financial landscape and prompting a reassessment of the United States' role on the international stage. Delving deeper into the complexities of the Bretton Woods system and its interactions with geopolitical dynamics reveals that the pursuit of economic interests was inextricably linked to broader political objectives. Understanding this symbiotic relationship is essential to unravelling the nuances of international affairs and the lasting implications of post-war economic reconstruction.

Victory and Consequences: Reassessing the Role of the United States on the World Stage

Following the climax of the Second World War and the establishment of the Bretton Woods system, there was a profound reassessment of the United States' role on the world stage. The interaction between economic power and geopolitical interests that shaped the post-war landscape is exciting.

The Allied powers' victory necessitated a complete restructuring of global dynamics, in which the United States emerged as a pre-eminent influence. Economically, the United States wielded unprecedented influence, using its resources to shape international financial mechanisms and support the reconstruction efforts of war-torn nations. This convergence of economic power and strategic political positioning solidified the United States' status as a central player in the global power rebalancing. Furthermore, the post-war period necessitated a thorough examination of the United States' moral and ethical responsibilities as it assumed its new global leadership.

The interplay of ideology, economic imperatives and global leadership responsibilities required a realignment of political paradigms in Washington. This chapter examined the complexities and dilemmas faced by policymakers as they sought to balance national interests with the common good, while leveraging the economic superiority gained during the war. The geopolitical ramifications of this reassessment are paramount as they reflect the complex interplay between diplomatic manoeuvring and economic advantages. The United States' rise to power required a delicate balance between asserting its authority and maintaining global stability, thrusting policymakers into a context fraught with challenges and opportunities. Through an incisive political lens, this chapter examines the lasting repercussions of victory, guiding readers through the intricate web of decisions and negotiations that defined the United States' global trajectory after the war.

3
The Post-War order and the Promise of the United Nations
American Leadership in World Peace

Laying the foundations for a new world order

The post-war period paved the way for the establishment of a new international order led by the United States and centred on stability and security. During this pivotal period, institutions such as the International Monetary Fund (IMF) and the World Bank were established to stabilise the global economy and support nations torn apart by war. The 1944 Bretton Woods Conference played a pivotal role in shaping these economic powers, primarily to prevent a recurrence of the economic downturns that had contributed to the previous global conflict. The United States' influence on the creation of these institutions was evident, reflecting its determination to shape the post-war world in accordance with its vision of stability and prosperity. Furthermore, the establishment of these organisations perpetuated the US monetary system as the linchpin of the international economic order. This gave the United States considerable influence in international financial affairs, enabling it to leverage its economic power to advance its geopolitical interests.

The economic foundations laid during this period clearly helped consolidate the United States' influence on the world stage, highlighting the complex relationship between economic power and geopolitical dominance. The United States' strategic positioning in the formation of these economic powers reflects its deeply rooted motivation to assert its dominance, both economically and geopolitically. It used financial institutions to promote its political objectives under the guise of global peace and prosperity. This interplay between economic hegemony and geopolitical influence has shaped the post-war international relations landscape, casting a shadow over subsequent diplomatic efforts.

Economic powers: financing peace and prosperity

In the aftermath of World War II, the global landscape was redrawn by political realignments and the economic power of nations seeking to assert their influence on the international stage. The United States emerged as a dominant economic power, backed by its vast industrial capacity and unrivalled wealth. This economic might translate into significant influence in international affairs, enabling the United States to reconstruct war-ravaged economies and establish new economic institutions to support global stability. The establishment of the Bretton Woods system was a pivotal moment in this endeavour, with economic hegemony becoming crucial for securing American interests and promoting a vision of peace and prosperity worldwide. The strategic deployment of financial resources and the imposition of economic policies played a decisive role in promoting US geopolitical objectives, often serving as a means of extending its sphere of influence while presenting a façade of altruism and cooperation.

Financing peace and prosperity became intertwined with the pursuit of self-interest, with economic aid and development assistance being used to forge alliances, counter ideological rivals and secure access to vital resources. The

Marshall Plan, for instance, exemplified the use of financial aid as a diplomatic tool to contain the spread of communism and rebuild war-torn European nations within a framework that served American economic and strategic interests. Institutions such as the International Monetary Fund (IMF) and the World Bank further reinforced US economic hegemony by allowing financial mechanisms to be manipulated to advance political objectives and enforce compliance by recipient countries.

This highlights the complex interaction between finance, foreign policy, and international relations, revealing the depth of calculation and pragmatism inherent in the pursuit of global primacy.

It is crucial to decipher the complex web of economic motivations underlying policies that are presented as benevolent and philanthropic, recognising the interplay of interests and power dynamics that guide decision-making on the world stage.

Bretton Woods and economic hegemony

The Bretton Woods Agreement, concluded in 1944, marked a turning point in the history of international finance and economic diplomacy. At the heart of this historic event was the establishment of a new monetary order aimed at promoting global economic stability and preventing a repeat of the devastating economic turmoil that characterised the interwar period. The United States, having emerged as the preeminent power after World War II, played a pivotal role in shaping the post-war economic landscape to advance its strategic interests.

The agreement paved the way for the establishment of pivotal organisations such as the International Monetary Fund (IMF) and the World Bank. These institutions were designed to foster international monetary cooperation and encourage long-term investment in the reconstruction and development of war-torn economies. This initiative was based on the United States' ambition to foster a post-war global environment that would be conducive to its economic and geopolitical interests.

It is important to recognise the link between economic dominance and national security objectives. The dominance of the US dollar as the world's primary reserve currency after Bretton Woods gave the nation considerable influence over global financial systems. By anchoring the international monetary system to the dollar, the United States strengthened its economic power and its ability to shape the rules of international trade and investment.

Furthermore, the Bretton Woods system enabled American multinational corporations and financial institutions to expand globally, strengthening the United States' economic presence in strategically important regions. This economic power translated into increased political influence for the United States, establishing it as a dominant player on the international stage. Behind the façade of promoting multilateral cooperation were the strategic imperatives of preserving American economic supremacy and consolidating US leadership in the post-war world order. The decisions made at Bretton Woods reflect the complex interplay of economic policy, power dynamics and geopolitical considerations, highlighting the ongoing significance of the conference's outcomes in shaping the current international economic landscape.

Geopolitical chessboard: the strategic positioning of the United States

We must now attempt to comprehend the intricate web of geopolitical interests that shapes global politics. After the Second World War, the United States emerged as a superpower and meticulously crafted its foreign policy to promote its strategic objectives and economic interests globally. This positioning on the global chessboard was motivated not only by ideological fervour, but also by a pragmatic and often ruthless pursuit of power and influence.

At the heart of this strategic calculation was the pursuit of economic domination and the perpetuation of American hegemony. Geopolitical considerations led the United States to establish military bases in strategic locations worldwide, creating a network through which to project power and influence. These bases served as symbols of American military might and acted as levers to exert pressure and obtain economic advantages. Control of vital sea lanes, natural resources and strategic locations was thus essential for protecting American economic interests and projecting power across continents.

Furthermore, establishing diplomatic relations and strong alliances with countries located at key geopolitical crossroads allowed the United States to consolidate its influence and secure favourable trade relations. Through economic aid, investment incentives and strategic partnerships, the United States sought to create a global economic sphere aligned with its own interests, leveraging its economic power to cultivate alliances and shape the international order. Additionally, the United States has skilfully used international financial institutions and multilateral organisations to strengthen its economic influence.

By leveraging its economic dominance, it has oriented these institutions to primarily serve its own interests, shaping global economic policies and ensuring its economic agenda occupies a central place in international affairs. Covert and overt interventions in foreign countries to protect economic interests and curb the spread of competing ideologies cannot be ignored.

CIA-backed coups, support for friendly dictators and military interventions were motivated by economic imperatives and the desire to maintain strategic influence over regions that were either rich in resources or critical to trade routes. In conclusion, the United States' strategic positioning on the geopolitical chessboard during the post-war period was a multifaceted endeavour, driven by deeply rooted economic and geopolitical considerations. Understanding this positioning is crucial to comprehending the broader motivations behind US foreign policy decisions and their lasting impact on global affairs.

The United Nations: A Platform for American Ideals

Following the devastation of World War II, the United Nations emerged as a beacon of hope for global cooperation and peace. For the United States, the UN presented an unprecedented opportunity to shape the post-war world order in accordance with American ideals and interests. Leveraging its economic and military might, the US sought to use the UN to promote democratic governance, human rights and market economies. At the same time, however, American policymakers recognised the UN's potential as a forum in which to advance economic and geopolitical strategies under the guise of humanitarian and security initiatives. The United States' financial power has enabled it to exert considerable influence within the UN system by utilising aid, loans, and development assistance to secure the necessary support for achieving its diplomatic and economic objectives.

Furthermore, the United States played a pivotal role in establishing the Bretton Woods institutions, including the International Monetary Fund and the World Bank, to consolidate American economic dominance within the context of international cooperation. Geopolitically, the UN provided a platform for the United States to demonstrate its leadership, rally its allies, and build global consensus around its strategic positioning — particularly in countering Soviet expansionism during the Cold War.

This allowed the United States to form a coalition of nations that supported its political objectives, presenting itself as the spearhead of collective security and peace. However, as the UN evolved, criticism emerged regarding the extent to which American interests guided its institutional mechanisms, raising questions about the disparities between professed ideals and self-serving policies. The tension between using the UN to promote American values and exploiting it to consolidate US economic and geopolitical influence highlights the complex dynamics that define America's engagement with the organisation. This chapter explores the multifaceted nature of American involvement in the United Nations, highlighting the complex intersections between ideology, power, and interests that have shaped American foreign policy on the global diplomatic stage.

Dollar diplomacy: aid, loans, and control

In the aftermath of World War II's devastation, the United States emerged as a global superpower with the economic power to shape the post-war world order. Central to its international strategy was the concept of 'dollar diplomacy', whereby it used its economic influence and financial aid to promote its geopolitical interests. This astute approach enabled the United States to exert influence on a global scale, shaping reconstruction efforts in war-torn Europe and beyond. Aid and loans were powerful tools, enabling the United States to project its economic power and embed its political objectives in recipient countries.

The Marshall Plan, the flagship programme of the dollar diplomacy framework, embodied this strategy perfectly. Designed as a comprehensive initiative to stimulate European recovery, it aimed to rebuild devastated economies while ensuring that this recovery aligned with American interests. By providing substantial financial assistance to Western European countries, the United States aimed to establish stable, prosperous democracies that would act as a barrier against communist expansion. The Marshall Plan effectively linked economic aid to political alignment, thereby consolidating US influence in the region and countering the Soviet Union's influence. Furthermore, the establishment of international financial institutions such as the World Bank and the International Monetary Fund (IMF) reinforced the scope of dollar diplomacy.

Through these entities, the United States was able to exert considerable influence over borrowing countries, often imposing political reforms and economic restructuring in exchange for financial support. This further emphasised the connection between economic aid and strategic objectives, strengthening American dominance in the global economy. However, while dollar diplomacy enabled the United States to extend its influence and promote its vision for the post-war world, it also raised ethical and sovereignty issues. Critics argued that imposing American economic policies and strict conditions on aid and loans infringed the autonomy of recipient countries, creating a climate of dependency and subservience. Furthermore, prioritising American interests in aid allocation led to accusations of neo-colonial practices and self-serving agendas.

Nevertheless, from a realist perspective, dollar diplomacy exemplified the pragmatic exercise of power in international relations. It demonstrated how economic tools can be utilised to serve national interests, revealing the intricate relationships between financial aid, geopolitical control, and policy alignment. As the Cold War unfolded, dollar diplomacy emerged as a defining feature of American foreign policy, highlighting the profound impact of economic power on global dynamics.

The Marshall Plan: Rebuilding Europe in the Interests of the United States

In the aftermath of World War II, Europe lay in ruins, its economies destroyed and millions of people in need of assistance. Against this challenging backdrop, the United States unveiled the Marshall Plan: a groundbreaking initiative aimed at revitalising war-torn Europe. While often regarded as an act of generosity, the Marshall Plan was not solely motivated by altruism. At its core, it served as a strategic tool to promote US economic and geopolitical interests while preventing the spread of communism. By providing massive financial aid totalling more than $12 billion (£9.2 billion), equivalent to approximately $130 billion (£101 billion) in today's dollars, the United States was able to extend its influence and consolidate its position as a global superpower.

By helping to rebuild Europe, the United States sought to create stable and prosperous markets for its goods and services, thereby securing long-term economic benefits. At the same time, the plan aimed to counter the appeal of communism by offering an alternative path to socio-economic renewal based on democratic principles. Through aid grants and intra-regional cooperation, the United States strengthened its ties with European nations, fostering enduring alliances throughout the Cold War and beyond. The strategic dimension of the Marshall Plan emphasised the interdependence of economics and politics, demonstrating the close link between foreign policy and financial power. Widely hailed as a turning point in international relations, the Marshall Plan also reflected the calculated pursuit of American interests by leveraging economic aid to expand its sphere of influence and strengthen its global position.

Counterbalancing Soviet expansionism

With the memory of World War II still fresh in the minds of world leaders, there was a palpable sense of urgency to prevent Soviet influence from spreading in war-torn Europe. The emergence of the Soviet Union as a global superpower directly challenged American economic and geopolitical interests, prompting the United States to adopt a multifaceted strategy to counterbalance Soviet expansionism.

Economically, the United States leveraged its financial resources to rebuild Western European countries through initiatives such as the Marshall Plan. By investing considerable sums of money in the region, the United States aimed to promote economic recovery and create a bulwark against communism. This approach reflected American leaders' deeply held belief in the correlation between economic prosperity and political stability, as well as the close link between financial aid and political allegiance.

In geopolitical terms, the policy of containment emerged, based on the concept of limiting Soviet influence through military, economic and diplomatic means, as outlined by political scientist George F. Kennan. Military alliances such as NATO were formed to consolidate collective security and deter Soviet aggression, visibly demonstrating America's commitment to preserving stability in Europe.

Furthermore, promoting democratic principles and free market economies not only contrasted with the Soviet system but also reinforced American dominance and influence. The Truman Doctrine became the cornerstone of American foreign policy, explicitly expressing a commitment to supporting nations threatened by communist subversion.

Although seemingly formulated in terms of ideological defence, this doctrine was closely linked to safeguarding economic interests and preventing the erosion of Western capitalist markets. It created a practical discourse fusing moral obligation with economic and strategic imperatives, further emphasising the multifaceted nature of American global engagement.

In retrospect, it is evident that countering Soviet expansionism was not merely an ideological confrontation; it was also deeply rooted in securing economic advantages, expanding market access and consolidating geopolitical influence. Consequently, the political decisions and strategic initiatives adopted by the United States were a calculated effort to leverage the power of money, influence new geopolitical landscapes, and advance long-term economic interests through containment.

The military-industrial complex: defence spending as a diplomatic tool

The military-industrial complex is an integral part of the modern political and economic landscape, exerting considerable influence over domestic and foreign policymaking. Following the Second World War, close collaboration between the government and the defence industry became a vital means of promoting American geopolitical interests. Defence spending, often presented as vital to national security, strengthens military capabilities and has significant diplomatic implications.

The economic power of the defence sector is immense, encompassing a vast network of industries that drive innovation, employ millions of people, and contribute substantially to the national GDP. At the heart of the military-industrial complex lies the intertwining of financial interests and political decisions. Defence companies have considerable financial resources at their disposal, enabling them to significantly influence legislators and policymakers. This influence is evident through lobbying efforts, campaign contributions, strategic partnerships and alliances with key government officials, all of which shape defence policy and procurement decisions. The economic implications of defence spending extend beyond corporate profit margins to permeate regional economies and labour markets, providing direct and indirect employment opportunities and further enhancing their influence.

On the global stage, defence spending is a critical diplomatic instrument that reflects and shapes foreign policy objectives. Military aid and arms sales are often employed to forge alliances, project power, and exert influence in strategically important regions. Furthermore, defence contracts and technology transfers strengthen ties with allied nations and cultivate spheres of influence. The strategic export of military equipment can create dependencies and relationships that extend far beyond simple transactions, significantly impacting diplomatic dynamics and power structures on the international stage.

Faced with calls to increase defence budgets to maintain national security, policymakers must make difficult decisions about how to allocate resources. Striking a balance between defence preparedness imperatives and broader national interests requires navigating complex geopolitical terrain. It should be noted that prioritising defence spending can overshadow other critical areas, such as infrastructure, education, and healthcare. Moreover, increased militarisation could inadvertently exacerbate international tensions, trigger arms races, and fuel conflicts, thereby hindering the pursuit of lasting global peace and stability.

In essence, the military–industrial complex's use of defence spending as a diplomatic tool embodies the complex interplay between economic imperatives, geopolitical strategy, and national security. This highlights the multifaceted nature of contemporary policymaking, forcing policymakers to balance the influence of special interest groups with broader national and international considerations.

The dilemma for policymakers: balancing national interests and global peace

Striking this delicate balance is an ongoing challenge. The complex web of economic, geopolitical and strategic considerations is intertwined with the relentless pursuit of power and influence on the world stage. In this complex landscape, money emerges as a central force that shapes foreign policy decisions. The allocation of defence spending, for example, is seen as a diplomatic tool that influences the dynamics of international relations. Economic prosperity and hegemony are inextricably linked to military power, exacerbating the dilemma faced by policymakers. Geopolitical interests further complicate the policymaking process. The quest to safeguard and promote national interests often intersects with broader initiatives for global peace.

The geopolitical chessboard is littered with strategic alliances, territorial disputes and regional power struggles, all of which require careful navigation. These manoeuvres are underpinned by multifaceted economic interests that compel nations to manoeuvre within an ever-changing international arena. The intersection of economic interests and geopolitical strategies is evident in the intricate diplomatic manoeuvring within international organisations such as the United Nations. Member states assert their influence by leveraging their financial contributions and resource allocation to advance their objectives. This intersection of power, money and diplomacy highlights the challenges faced by policymakers who must balance national ambitions with the need for global peace. Furthermore, striking a balance between promoting national economic growth and maintaining global stability requires astute policymaking.

The intricacies of economic interdependence and the pursuit of bilateral and multilateral trade agreements highlight the challenges policymakers face in reconciling national economic interests with the need for global peace. The considerable ramifications of these economic decisions extend beyond international borders, underscoring the inherent tension between promoting national interests and fostering global harmony. To resolve this dilemma, policymakers must methodically evaluate priorities and discern points of convergence or conflict between national interests and the broader pursuit of global peace. The dilemma persists as decisions made at the national level have repercussions for the global geopolitical landscape, creating a perpetual struggle to strike a balance that preserves national prosperity without hindering progress towards a more peaceful world. It is in this complex balancing act that the actual test of leadership and governance lies. Indeed, striking this balance remains a critical challenge for policymakers navigating the complexities of international relations.

4
The Birth of Israel and the Truman Doctrine
A Colonial Fact

The beginnings of a new state: early Zionist aspirations and global reactions

Emerging in the late 19th century, the Zionist movement sought to establish a national homeland for the Jewish people in the historic territory of Palestine. This movement grew during a period of rising nationalism and aspirations for self-determination, ideas that resonated deeply within the broader global context. At the heart of these early Zionist aspirations was the desire to create a sanctuary for Jewish communities, given the profound impact of historical persecution and anti-Semitic sentiments on Jewish populations in various countries. However, this quest for a national home was intertwined with complex political dynamics as it involved navigating the interests and concerns of multiple stakeholders, both nationally and internationally. The international community responded with a mixture of enthusiasm, scepticism and apprehension. While some viewed the Zionist vision as a reaffirmation of fundamental human rights and a means of redressing historical injustices, others saw it as a disruptive force that could fuel regional tensions and undermine existing socio-political structures.

The question of Zionism's compatibility with the local Arab population and its national aspirations added an extra layer of complexity to the unfolding narrative. As diplomatic efforts unfolded and the geopolitical landscape shifted, economic and strategic interests began to influence the overall discourse significantly.

Financial resources and economic considerations emerged as determining factors in the responses of powerful nations. Furthermore, the lingering echoes of the First World War and the subsequent reconfiguration of global power dynamics emphasised the intricate relationship between international politics and strategic objectives. Underlying reasons closely tied to economic and geopolitical interests played a crucial role in shaping policy formulation and diplomatic engagements around the Zionist cause. Consequently, studying early Zionist aspirations and the range of global responses necessitates an understanding of the interaction between ideology, power dynamics and international relations.

Truman's dilemma: balancing political pressure and personal convictions

President Harry S. Truman faced a significant dilemma when it came to recognising and supporting Israel. As a leader grappling with the complexities of post-war geopolitics, he found himself torn between political pressure from various interest groups and his deeply held personal convictions. On the one hand, influential voices advocated for the swift recognition and support of the fledgling State of Israel, leveraging their networks of power and money to influence policy in their favour. The Zionist cause had garnered considerable attention and support through diplomatic channels and lobbying efforts that secured substantial financial contributions. These funding networks played a central role in shaping the discourse on American foreign policy, adding to the complexity of Truman's decision-making process. At the same time, Truman was torn between his personal convictions and his moral compass, which led him to sympathise with the Jewish people's aspirations for self-determination and security following the atrocities of the Holocaust.

The tension between these competing forces, influenced by economic and geopolitical interests, created a challenging environment for Truman, who was striving to strike a delicate balance. The economic implications of supporting or refusing to recognise the nascent state of Israel were closely linked to broader global considerations.

Israel's strategic positioning in the unstable Middle East, at the heart of regional power dynamics and with access to vital trade routes, has significant geopolitical implications. Furthermore, the ethical dimensions of American policy were under intense scrutiny, with implications for the United States' position as a champion of freedom and justice on the world stage. Truman's dilemma perfectly illustrates the complex interplay between domestic pressures, international ramifications and personal principles in the formulation of foreign policy. This chapter delves into Truman's multifaceted decision-making process, emphasising the interplay between power politics, economic interests, and moral imperatives during this pivotal period in history.

Lobbyists and dollars: the funding networks that shape policy

The intricate web of lobbyists and funding networks played a pivotal role in shaping US foreign policy, particularly concerning the establishment of Israel and the Truman Doctrine. Lobbyists representing various interests, including those aligned with Zionist causes, exert considerable influence over policymakers through financial contributions, strategic alliances and persuasive advocacy.

At the heart of these networks are powerful interest groups that leverage their financial resources to influence policy outcomes. These organisations employ a variety of tactics, ranging from direct contributions to election campaigns to sustained efforts to secure favourable policies. By strategically allocating funds and employing savvy lobbyists, these groups can advance their agendas and secure access to influential figures within the political establishment. This influence extends beyond mere persuasion, often encroaching on the realm of policy formulation and implementation. Furthermore, economic and geopolitical interests converge in this sphere of influence, adding another layer of complexity to the dynamic.

As geopolitical shifts and strategic alliances unfold, lobbying efforts become increasingly intertwined with broader global developments. The interaction between economic imperatives and geopolitical strategies underscores the substantial impact that lobbying and financial networks have on foreign policy decisions. Moreover, the interconnected nature of lobbying and financial networks emphasises the intricate connections between domestic and international affairs. Ethnic and religious groups in the United States, particularly those advocating pro-Israeli interests, have proven adept at leveraging their political capital to influence foreign policy decisions. Thus, the intersection of domestic ethnic politics and international affairs amplifies the influence of financial and lobbying networks on policy formulation and implementation. To navigate this complex landscape, policymakers must contend with the intertwined forces of financial influence, geopolitical imperatives and domestic political dynamics. Understanding the complex interplay of these factors is crucial for grasping the underlying mechanisms that guided the foreign policy decisions surrounding the establishment of Israel and the development of the Truman Doctrine.

Ethnic politics at the national level: the influence of American Jews on foreign policy

The significant influence of ethnic politics, particularly that of the American Jewish community, on the formulation of American foreign policy cannot be ignored. This influence is closely linked to lobbying, funding networks and strategic interests. It is important to recognise that the American Jewish community has historically played a pivotal role in advocating for policies that align with Israel's interests, which frequently align with the broader geopolitical and economic objectives of the United States.

The influence of money on foreign policymaking cannot be overstated. American Jewish individuals and organisations have been very active in making financial contributions to political campaigns and lobbying efforts. These contributions have given them access to policymakers, enabling them to advocate effectively for policies that align with their perceived interests. Beyond financial influence, the deep historical and emotional ties between the American Jewish community and Israel have also played a crucial role in shaping foreign policy decisions. Shared cultural and religious ties have fostered a sense of solidarity and commitment to supporting Israel within the community, further amplifying its influence on foreign policy.

Furthermore, the alignment of Israeli interests with broader US geopolitical and economic objectives creates an environment in which advocating for Israel-friendly policies is often framed as being in line with US national interests. This convergence of interests means that American Jewish influence on foreign policy is motivated not only by ethnic ties but also by a strategic alignment with perceived US interests. Moreover, Israel's strategic importance in the Middle East, both geopolitically and economically, has strengthened the American Jewish community's influence in shaping US foreign policy even further.

The region's geostrategic importance, including access to vital resources and countering regional adversaries, has led to a convergence of interests between the US government and pro-Israel advocates within the American Jewish community. This has strengthened lobbying efforts and the influence of American Jews on policies related to the Middle East and beyond. In conclusion, the interaction between financial contributions, historical and emotional ties, and strategic alignment with broader American interests highlights the significant impact of the American Jewish community on US foreign policy. Understanding these dynamics is crucial for comprehending the multifaceted factors that influence foreign policy decisions, underscoring the complex interplay between domestic ethnic politics and global geopolitical considerations.

Economic leverage and post-war reconstruction: aid, trade and strategic interests

In the aftermath of World War II, the world's significant powers found themselves at a historic turning point. The war-torn landscape offered an unprecedented opportunity to shape the post-war world order, with economic leverage playing a central role. As the United States emerged as a dominant force on the international stage, its economic power became a key instrument for advancing its strategic interests and influencing foreign policy decisions.

Post-war reconstruction aid was one of the primary means by which the United States exerted its economic influence. By providing financial assistance to war-torn nations, the United States sought to facilitate recovery and foster alliances that aligned with its geopolitical interests. This strategic deployment of economic resources helped consolidate political ties and promote policies favourable to the United States in recipient countries. Furthermore, trade relations became a crucial element of post-war diplomacy, with the United States leveraging its economic weight to negotiate favourable terms that would strengthen its position on the world stage. Through trade agreements and partnerships, the United States sought to promote its economic interests while strengthening its geopolitical position.

However, behind the façade of humanitarian aid and economic cooperation lay deeper motivations rooted in realpolitik. Aid allocation and trade agreement structuring were meticulously designed to serve the United States' broader strategic objectives, often at the expense of the sovereignty and autonomy of other nations. Geopolitical considerations heavily influenced the distribution of aid and the formulation of trade policies, with recipient countries being manoeuvred into positions that favoured American hegemony.

In this complex web of economic interactions, power relations were underpinned by the pursuit of national interests, thus shaping the contours of the post-war world order. Here, we examine the multiple dimensions of economic influence, exploring the interactions among aid, trade, and strategic interests. The objective is to reveal the underlying motivations and implications of economic policies in the context of political power games, emphasising the delicate balance between humanitarian goals and geopolitical considerations.

A moral imperative? A narrative that ignored the rights of the Palestinian people

Following the end of the Second World War, the world was confronted with the horrific revelations of the Holocaust, in which the Nazi regime systematically exterminated six million Jews and millions of others. This unprecedented genocide left indelible scars on humanity and raised profound moral and ethical questions. A global awakening marked the post-war period as nations grappled with the weight of history and sought to understand their respective roles in preventing such atrocities. For the United States, the haunting spectre of the Holocaust gave a moral dimension to its foreign policy decisions. However, the strategic positioning of the United States in the aftermath of the war conflicted with the urgent need to respond to the plight of Holocaust and other genocide survivors. The memory of the Holocaust compelled policymakers to consider the ethics of international relations, alongside the geopolitical calculations of the emerging Cold War era.

Although the United States had a deep and sincere concern for the victims of the Holocaust, this moral imperative was often intertwined with the complex web of economic and geopolitical interests that shaped foreign policy. Furthermore, the establishment of Israel as a cornerstone following the Holocaust created a connection between historical narratives, moral obligations, and strategic considerations.

However, behind this moral aspect lay a set of economic considerations and geopolitical interests. The plight of Holocaust survivors reverberated through the corridors of power, where lobbying efforts, financial contributions and diplomatic manoeuvring intertwined with ideological alliances and strategic priorities. Thus, the legacy of the Holocaust transcended the realm of pure morality, becoming intertwined with the currents of realpolitik and the dynamics of global power. The subsequent chapter of history reveals the complex interplay between moral imperatives, economic interests, and geopolitical strategies — a confluence that continues to resonate in the annals of international relations. Most importantly, throughout this entire affair, the historical rights of the Arab population of Palestine were not considered.

The partition of Palestine: diplomatic manoeuvring at the United Nations

In the aftermath of the Second World War, the geopolitical landscape transformed, giving rise to significant diplomatic manoeuvring at the United Nations concerning the creation of Israel. The balance of power within the UN and among its member states significantly influenced the outcome of this historic decision. Economic and geopolitical interests were closely intertwined in the debates and negotiations that ultimately led to the creation of the State of Israel. The competing agendas of the major powers, particularly the United States and the Soviet Union, added an extra layer of complexity to the proceedings. Against a backdrop of Western support for the establishment of a Jewish homeland and the horrors of the Holocaust, the moral imperative to create Israel became a focal point of UN deliberations.

However, behind this humanitarian concern lay strategic considerations that influenced the positions of various countries. Economic ties and potential alliances in the Middle East region guided many countries within the UN. Additionally, powerful lobbying efforts and financial influence played significant roles in these negotiations.

Backed by substantial financial resources and a skilled network of supporters, the Zionist lobby exerted considerable pressure on key decision-makers within the United Nations. This dynamic highlighted the intersection of money, political influence, and foreign policy —a dynamic that would continue to shape international relations in the years to come. As the discussions progressed, it became clear that the establishment of Israel would have profound implications that extended far beyond the immediate geopolitical context. The broader rivalry between the Western bloc and the Soviet sphere of influence infused the debate with underlying ideological currents, further complicating the path to resolution. The intersection of economic interests and superpower rivalry emphasised the multifaceted nature of the decisions made at the UN.

Ultimately, diplomatic manoeuvring culminated in the historic UN General Assembly resolution of 29 November 1947, which approved the partition of Palestine into two states: a Jewish state and an Arab state. This momentous decision represented the convergence of Zionist political interests, geopolitical calculations, and economic considerations on the international stage.

The establishment of Israel as a 'Zionist national' entity reflected the complex interplay of Western hegemonic aspirations and financial interests, as well as their enduring influence on global policymaking. However, it is important to note that this was achieved by obliterating the right of the Palestinian people to live on their ancestral lands. Consequently, from the outset, Israel was an imperialist outpost and a symbol of Western colonialism, unwilling to acknowledge its historic defeat around the world.

Jewish money: contributions and election campaigns in the United States

The intertwining of money, politics, and power lies at the

heart of the American democratic process. In the American electoral landscape, financial links exert significant influence on election results and political priorities. The influx of election contributions from various interest groups, including corporations, special interest lobbies and wealthy individuals, effectively shapes the trajectory of political campaigns and legislative agendas. Within the labyrinth of political financing, economic and geopolitical interests are closely intertwined. Corporations and industry associations strategically allocate substantial resources to fund political candidates who pledge to defend their business objectives and regulatory preferences.

This fusion of financial support and policymaking can raise concerns about the integrity of decision-making processes. Elected officials may indeed feel indebted to their benefactors, which can compromise the public interest in favour of private interests. Furthermore, geopolitical considerations play a central role in the financing of election campaigns within this financial nexus. Foreign entities and governments, driven by their strategic objectives, may seek to influence US elections by providing financial support to candidates who are favourable to their geopolitical ambitions. Such interventions compromise the autonomy of the electoral system and complicate US foreign policy, as the interaction between financial support and diplomatic alignments blurs the distinction between domestic politics and international relations.

The implications of this financial link extend beyond the electoral sphere to the corridors of politics and governance. Elected officials, aware of the substantial resources at stake, may prioritise the demands of their financial backers over the general welfare of their constituents. Consequently, policies relating to taxation, trade, environmental regulation and healthcare often reflect the specific interests of well-funded entities, perpetuating disparities in economic opportunity and social welfare. Analysing the interdependence of money, influence, and politics is therefore essential to understanding the complex mechanisms that govern the American democratic system. Examining the deep economic and geopolitical motivations behind campaign financing reveals the complexity and challenges involved in preserving the fundamental principles of democratic governance. As the financial nexus continues to exert its pervasive influence, safeguarding the integrity of elections and policymaking in the United States becomes a task of the utmost importance that requires scrutiny and strategic reforms.

The Shadow of Empire: British Withdrawal and American Ascendance

As the sun began to set on the British Empire, a new era of power dynamics was about to emerge. The process of decolonisation brought significant changes to global geopolitics, with the United States strategically positioning itself to fill the void left by the British withdrawal. The transfer of power from colonial authorities to emerging sovereign nations created a complex environment in which economic and geopolitical interests intersected with the growing tensions of the Cold War.

Economically, the British Empire's withdrawal presented the United States with an opportunity to expand its sphere of influence. As former colonies sought stability and development, the United States leveraged its economic resources to forge trade agreements that would lay the foundation for long-term partnerships. This economic rise also had significant financial repercussions, with capital flows and investments playing a pivotal role in the post-colonial landscape. The geopolitical ramifications of the British withdrawal were equally profound.

As British imperialism declined, the United States became increasingly involved in the affairs of regions formerly under colonial rule. The strategic importance of these territories in the context of the emerging rivalry between the United States and the Soviet Union during the Cold War prompted American policymakers to actively participate in reshaping the political architectures of newly independent states. The struggle for influence and ideological alignment in these regions became a key aspect of American foreign policy, resulting in both overt and covert interventions aimed at asserting dominance.

Furthermore, the vacuum created by the British withdrawal led to a reconfiguration of alliances and allegiances. The need for security and stability during the transition to independence provided the United States with a favourable opportunity to forge new alliances with emerging leaders, thereby amplifying its reach and influence on the international stage. This network of alliances projected American influence and served as a counterweight to perceived threats from rival powers, strengthening the foundations of

American supremacy. Thus, the shadow cast by the declining British Empire paved the way for the ascendancy of the United States, marking a decisive turning point in world politics. The interplay of economic incentives, geopolitical manoeuvring and the quest for supremacy shaped the trajectory of American foreign policy during this transitional period, setting the stage for the defining ideological battles and emerging alliances that characterised the early Cold War.

Setting the stage for the Cold War: ideological battles and emerging alliances

Once the dust had settled after the Second World War, a new global landscape emerged, defined by ideological confrontation and the consolidation of power blocs. Former allies in the fight against fascism, the United States and the Soviet Union found themselves engaged in a struggle for dominance, propelling the world into the Cold War era. This ideological battle was not only a clash of political ideals but was also closely linked to economic and geopolitical interests, with profound implications for international relations. The concept of containment became central to American foreign policy, with policymakers seeking to curb the spread of communism and expand the sphere of capitalist influence.

Economic considerations played a pivotal role in determining the allocation of resources and shaping diplomatic initiatives. The formation of strategic alliances and regional partnerships became a vital means of promoting American interests and exerting influence on the global stage. Backed by financial and military support, these alliances served to consolidate power and counter the perceived threat of communist expansion. The leading players on this geopolitical chessboard used their economic influence to sway the allegiances of nations, engaging in a complex web of negotiations and transactions to form a coalition against Soviet influence. The intertwining of economic and political factors emphasised the multifaceted nature of international relations during this period.

Furthermore, the emerging arms race between the United States and the Soviet Union heightened the importance of economic resources, as military capabilities became inextricably linked to economic power. The competition for technological superiority and military dominance had profound economic repercussions, stimulating significant spending and innovation in defence industries. This approach reshaped the dynamics of global power and reinforced the embedding of economic interests in the fabric of Cold War policymaking. As the international community faced the spectre of nuclear confrontation and mounting tensions, the connection between economic imperatives and political strategies became more apparent. This complex interplay of economic power, geopolitical manoeuvring and ideological conflicts defined the complex landscape of Cold War diplomacy, highlighting the enduring influence of monetary resources and economic motivations throughout history.

5
Cold War Calculations
Israel, a Destabilising Factor for Stabilising the Region

The geopolitical chessboard: American Strategies in the Middle East

During the Cold War, the Middle East was considered a crucial arena for the United States, with Israel emerging as a strategic pawn. Located at the crossroads of Europe, Asia, and Africa, Israel's geographical position offered the United States a gateway through which to influence and control regional dynamics. Its Mediterranean coastline provided access to vital trade routes and naval bases, enabling the United States to project its power into the heart of the Arab world. Furthermore, its borders with hostile Arab states made Israel an attractive ally for containing Soviet expansion and blocking pro-Soviet regimes. The Suez Canal, a vital artery of world trade, reinforced the strategic importance of Israel's location, prompting the United States to ensure favourable regional conditions.

The vast oil reserves of the Middle East and their role in fuelling the global economy further amplified the United States' interest in maintaining stability and a regime whose raison d'être is to serve American strategic interests in the region. This has led the United States to provide Israel with military aid, economic assistance and unconditional diplomatic support, viewing it as an extension of the American dream of global hegemony and a reliable ally in safeguarding US interests.

The convergence of economic and geopolitical interests

has prompted US policymakers to navigate the complex web of alliances and rivalries in the Middle East, positioning Israel as pivotal in their grand strategy against Soviet influence and the resurgence of Arab-Islamic nationalism. Thus, Israel's geographical location was strategically important during the Cold War, reshaping regional dynamics and influencing the global power game. This laid the foundations for the United States' lasting relationship with Israel.

Containment policy: navigating ideological battle lines

During the Cold War, the United States implemented a policy of containment aimed at preventing the spread of communism and Soviet influence. This policy strongly influenced American strategies in the Middle East, particularly regarding Israel.

Understanding the complex interaction between ideological imperatives, economic interests, and geopolitical considerations that shaped this policy is essential. The balance of power at the time was not limited to military might or diplomatic manoeuvring, but also revolved around significant financial investments and strategic alliances that underpinned American foreign policy objectives. The policy of containment required navigating unpredictable ideological battle lines, where perception was often as important as reality. The American government had to strike a delicate balance between supporting Israel and considering the broader regional situation, including Arab nationalism and the struggle against Soviet expansion. Economic and geopolitical interests were closely linked to the ideological struggle, resulting in a delicate game of power and influence.

The provision of military aid and the conclusion of arms agreements aimed at strengthening Israel's strategic position were motivated by the desire not only to counterbalance Soviet influence but also to protect economic assets and trade routes that were essential to American interests. In the Cold War era, decisions regarding containment policy were subject to intense pressure from various interest groups. The role of money and finance cannot be underestimated. Indeed, these elements played a central role in shaping US foreign policy towards Israel.

Furthermore, the sustained influence of pro-Israel lobby groups accentuated the intertwining of economic weight and ideological alignment even more. Even as the importance of containment waned, its legacy continued to reverberate in US foreign relations, leaving a lasting impact on the management of strategic alliances and ideological motivations. Navigating the ideological battle lines of the Cold War ultimately required an in-depth understanding of the intricate connections between economic, geopolitical and ideological factors. This combination continues to influence international relations to this day.

Military aid and arms sales: strengthening a strategic position

In the geopolitical theatre of the Cold War, military aid and arms agreements were essential for strengthening a strategic position in the Middle East. Recognising the region's importance as a battleground for ideological supremacy, the United States strengthened its alliance with Israel by providing sophisticated weaponry and military support. This initiative was driven by a convergence of economic and geopolitical interests, as well as a desire to counter Soviet influence and maintain dominance in this oil-rich region. Providing military aid and concluding arms agreements served to demonstrate the balance of power at stake, enabling the United States to consolidate its position as a key player in developing regional security agreements.

Through a complex network of alliances and partnerships, the United States strategically leveraged military aid to strengthen its ties with Israel, securing a reliable ally and erecting a bulwark against Soviet expansionism. From fighter jets and missile systems to intelligence cooperation and joint military exercises, military aid and arms contracts strengthened Israel's defence capabilities. They consolidated their pivotal role in the United States' strategy for regional stability.

Beyond the supply of weapons, these agreements were closely linked to economic considerations. They facilitated the maintenance of favourable trade relations and access to vital resources, including oil and strategic maritime trade routes. Furthermore, the transfer of military technology and equipment strengthened Israel's ability to ensure its own security and helped project US influence throughout the Middle East.

This symbiotic relationship, based on mutual strategic interests, enabled the United States to advance its geopolitical objectives while equipping Israel to defend itself in an environment made unstable and hostile by unfair Western policy towards the Palestinians. The multifaceted nature of military aid and arms agreements highlights the complex interplay between economic imperatives and geopolitical calculations during the Cold War. As the United States sought to contain Soviet expansion and protect its vital economic interests, strengthening Israel's military power became a central element of its overall strategy. Ultimately, this strategic alliance had lasting repercussions for the regional balance of power, shaping the trajectory of conflicts and alliances for decades to come.

Economic interests: oil, trade routes and regional stability

When examining the complex web of international relations during the Cold War, the central role played by economic interests in shaping geopolitical policies is not to be underestimated. In the Middle East, the quest for oil, control of trade routes and regional stability were the main factors influencing the United States' commitment to Israel as a strategic ally against Soviet influence. The importance of the region's oil resources to the global economy is undeniable. As the world's major industrial powers became increasingly dependent on Middle Eastern oil, ensuring access to these reserves became a key concern for the United States. The presence of vast oil reserves in the Middle East fuelled the desire to establish stable political arrangements that would guarantee reliable access to this vital resource. Furthermore, the strategic importance of trade routes, notably the Suez Canal, reinforced the United States' interest in the region. Recognising the economic implications of controlling key maritime passages, American policymakers sought to prevent these vital arteries of global commerce from falling under the control of adversarial forces.

Moreover, the quest for regional stability was closely linked to economic considerations. A destabilised Middle East would pose a direct threat to the flow of trade and oil, and therefore to the economic prosperity of the West. The paradox is that, on the one hand, a disruptive element is created in a region that has just emerged from colonisation. However, it is claimed that arming and strengthening this element will create stability.

It was in this context that US support for Israel took on a multifaceted dimension, motivated not only by real security concerns but also by the imperative need to preserve American economic interests. During the Cold War, the United States' alignment with Israel and Israel's alignment with the United States were not solely based on ideological affinities or shared democratic values; they were primarily a strategic calculation aimed at protecting and promoting American economic and geopolitical interests in the region. Thus, understanding the multiple economic motivations that underpinned American policy towards Israel during the Cold War reveals a dynamic in which financial imperatives intertwined with geopolitics to redefine the contours of global power dynamics.

Intelligence ties: sharing secrets in the shadow of the Iron Curtain

During the Cold War, the collaboration between American and Israeli intelligence services was pivotal in the struggle for global dominance. With the world divided along the ideological front lines of democracy and communism, the secret sharing of intelligence between the two allies became a strategic imperative. The power dynamics of these intelligence ties were deeply rooted in the economic and geopolitical interests that both nations sought to protect. The rise of the Soviet Union as a formidable adversary compelled the United States to forge close working relations with Israel in order to secure reliable allies in the Middle East.

This collaboration extended to intelligence, where both countries had a mutual interest in sharing classified information. From military strategies to technological developments, this exchange strengthened both nations' capabilities to confront the common threat posed by the Iron Curtain. The exchange of secrets between Washington and Tel Aviv also helped consolidate strategic alignment, ensuring the interests of both countries were closely linked.

While economic and geopolitical interests continued to underpin foreign policy decisions, this network of shared intelligence became essential to maintaining stability and countering Soviet influence in the region. Against the backdrop of the Cold War, intelligence cooperation between the

United States and Israel developed into a paramountly important tool, shaping the course of events on the world stage. This symbiotic relationship strengthened not only the security of both nations but also their broader agendas in their relentless quest for dominance amid the tumultuous geopolitics of the time. The close collaboration between American and Israeli intelligence services during the Cold War illustrates the intricate interplay of economic and geopolitical interests in international relations, shedding light on the multifaceted motivations underlying political decisions.

Delicate balance: supporting Israel in the face of rising Arab nationalism

The rise of Arab nationalism in the mid-20th century posed a significant challenge to American foreign policy in the Middle East. As Arab nations sought independence and self-determination, their assertiveness clashed with the United States' strategic alliance with Israel. Supporting Israel in this context required a nuanced understanding of the economic and geopolitical implications.

Economically, supporting Israel meant preserving access to vital regional resources and trade routes. The Suez Canal, a vital route for global trade, underscored the importance of US involvement in the Middle East. Therefore, ensuring stability and influence in this pivotal region became a significant concern for policymakers, compelling them to navigate the complexities of Israeli-Arab relations with caution.

Geopolitically, the United States recognised Israel as a valuable Cold War ally amid regional power dynamics. By supporting Israel, the United States aimed to counter the influence of Arab socialist movements aligned with the Soviet Union. This strategic positioning highlighted the intricate web of alliances and allegiances that shaped the political landscape at that time.

Furthermore, when formulating its approach to Israel and the Arab world, the United States was aware of the need to appease domestic pressures. Lobbying efforts by Israel's advocates exerted considerable influence on Capitol Hill, shaping policies and aid programmes designed to support the fledgling nation. Meanwhile, anti-colonialist rhetoric and solidarity with Arab states were gaining momentum within American society, further complicating the task of policymakers charged with managing divergent interests. This complex dance of diplomacy unfolded against the backdrop of the broader ideological struggle between capitalism and communism. The presence of natural resources, combined with the region's strategic importance, made the Middle East a key battleground in the Cold War's geopolitical game. In this context, every decision regarding American support for Israel was of profound importance, as it was intrinsically linked to the global confrontation between the superpowers.

Throughout history, the United States has faced the challenge of supporting Israel while navigating the rise of Arab nationalism with caution. The interplay of economic, geopolitical and domestic factors made it difficult to maintain balance amid competing interests and ideologies. Ultimately, the United States found itself caught in a high-stakes balancing act where every move had profound implications for the shifting balance of power and influence in the Middle East.

Influence of lobbying: directing Congressional support towards Israel

The influence of lobbying in directing US Congressional support towards Israel cannot be underestimated. A multitude of interest groups and individuals with economic, geopolitical, and ideological interests devote considerable resources to shaping the political landscape in favour of Israel. The power of money in influencing policymakers is a defining feature of this complex network. Lobbying entities provide financial support to candidates and elected officials, exerting considerable influence through campaign contributions and leveraging their economic clout to shape political outcomes. This intertwining of economic interests and political decisions has created a system in which lobbying funnels significant resources into cultivating relationships with policymakers and advancing agendas that align with Israel's interests. Furthermore, the deep-rooted economic and geopolitical ties between the United States and Israel are the foundation of this lobbying machine.

Beyond ideological support for Israel, a network of economic interdependencies and strategic partnerships motivates the considerable efforts to secure favourable policies. The defence industry, for instance, is one of the primary beneficiaries of the US–Israel relationship, enjoying substantial financial gains from arms contracts and military aid programmes. This symbiotic alliance is further strengthened by intelligence cooperation, where the exchange of strategic information reinforces mutual interests and consolidates lobbying efforts in Washington.

Moreover, the geopolitical context in the Middle East amplifies the importance of lobbying to secure Congressional support for Israel. In an unstable regional environment, Israel's perception as a stable democratic ally amidst a multitude of potential adversaries motivates lobbying efforts to shape public opinion and secure political support. By emphasising Israel's strategic value in such a region, lobbying entities present narratives that highlight the broader geopolitical implications of unwavering support for the nation. This framework aligns with US interests in maintaining stability in the Middle East and countering perceived threats, thereby fostering a mutually reinforcing cycle between lobbying influence and policy outcomes. The complex network of lobbying influence, closely linked to economic and geopolitical interests, shapes congressional support for Israel. Understanding the interaction between financial influence, strategic imperatives and narrative-building helps us to grasp the multifaceted dynamics that drive policymaking in the context of US–Israel relations.

Propaganda and perceptions: crafting a narrative against Soviet threats

During the Cold War, the United States skilfully crafted a

narrative portraying Israel as a bulwark against Soviet expansion in the Middle East. This strategic narrative was disseminated through various channels to garner domestic and international support for US involvement in the region. The perception of Israel as a crucial ally in curbing Soviet influence served to justify military aid and diplomatic support, profoundly shaping the geopolitical landscape. A key aspect of this narrative was presenting Israel as a democratic outpost surrounded by authoritarian regimes supported by the Soviet Union. By emphasising the shared values of democracy and freedom between the United States and Israel, policymakers positioned Israel as a natural partner in the fight against communist ideology. This narrative effectively reinforced the idea of a binary conflict between freedom and tyranny, while glossing over complex regional dynamics and historical grievances.

Additionally, the dissemination of propaganda material played a pivotal role in shaping perceptions of the Soviet threat in the Middle East. The US government sought to portray Soviet-backed entities in the region as existential threats not only to Israel, but also to American interests, through carefully selected messages. Various media, including newspapers, radio broadcasts and films, reinforced the image of Israel as a vulnerable yet steadfast democracy facing a threatening communist adversary, which became deeply ingrained in public consciousness. Economic considerations also underpinned the propaganda efforts, with the United States leveraging its economic power to reinforce Israel's image as a vital ally in the fight against Soviet influence.

Economic aid programmes were presented as vital investments in regional stability, based on the implicit understanding that a strong and secure Israel would act as a barrier to Soviet expansionism. Furthermore, economic relations with Israel became a powerful means of promoting American interests in the region, aligning economic incentives with broader geopolitical objectives. It is important to recognise that developing this narrative was not just about shaping public opinion. Instead, it reflected a sophisticated strategy aimed at consolidating American influence in the Middle East, protecting economic assets and countering perceived threats to national security. The intertwining of propaganda, perceptions, and economic and geopolitical imperatives underscores the complex web of motivations that guided American policy during the Cold War, leaving a lasting imprint on the region's trajectory.

Financial leverage: the power of economic aid programmes

Economic aid programmes have long been used as a tool for political leverage and influence, particularly in geopolitical power struggles. In the context of US–Israel relations during the Cold War, for example, economic aid played a critical role in cementing the strategic alliance between the two nations. An analysis of the reasons behind the allocation of economic aid reveals a complex web of interests that extends far beyond simple financial assistance. Fundamentally, the granting of economic aid was closely linked to broader geopolitical strategies aimed at countering Soviet influence in the Middle East.

The United States recognised Israel as a key partner in this endeavour, deploying economic aid to bolster the country's stability and security. This support helped nurture a strong alliance that aligned with the United States' overall goal of containing Soviet expansionism. Economic aid programmes provided tangible resources for Israel's development and cemented a bond based on shared strategic interests. The intertwining of economic and military aid further accentuated this dynamic, creating a comprehensive framework of support that positioned Israel as a key regional ally.

Examining the complex layers of economic aid reveals the intersection of economic and geopolitical motivations. The United States recognised Israel's thriving economy as a potential asset for promoting regional stability and American interests. By channelling financial resources to Israel, the United States aimed to create an environment conducive to its own economic interests, while also strengthening its relationship with a reliable partner in an unstable region. Furthermore, economic aid facilitated Israel's integration into the global economic framework, strengthening its ties with Western powers and consolidating its position as a bulwark against Soviet influence.

Beyond the economic realm, the provision of economic aid emphasised the United States' commitment to supporting a steadfast geopolitical ally. This strategic investment signalled a long-term commitment to a robust partnership, one that transcends short-term political considerations. The repercussions of this financial leverage are still being felt in contemporary US–Israel relations, shaping the enduring dynamic between the two nations. The legacy of economic aid as an essential tool for consolidating alliances provides valuable insight into the intricate relationship between power, money and politics, emphasising the multifaceted nature of international relations.

The Legacy of Cold War Alliances: Long-Term Implications for US–Israel Relations

The legacy of Cold War alliances has had profound and lasting implications for US–Israel relations. At the heart of this legacy lies a complex web of economic, geopolitical and strategic interests that continues to influence policy decisions and bilateral relations to this day. The economic aid provided by the United States to Israel during the Cold War was a manifestation of political support and served to consolidate Israel's position as a key ally in an unstable region. Furthermore, this economic aid was accompanied by deeper military cooperation and intelligence sharing, forming a symbiotic relationship aimed at countering Soviet influence in the region.

Israel's strategic importance as a bulwark against Soviet expansionism and the rise of Arab-Islamic nationalism cannot be overstated. American investment in Israel's military capabilities laid the foundation for a long-term alliance that extended beyond the Cold War. When the Cold War ended, the dynamics of US–Israel relations changed, but the legacy of this alliance endured. Economic and geopolitical interests continued to underpin US support for Israel, with economic aid and military assistance playing a pivotal role in sustaining a strategic presence in the region.

The close ties established during the Cold War were perpetuated through diplomatic and trade agreements, reflecting a mutual understanding of shared interests and goals. Beyond the economic and security dimensions, the Cold War alliance also shaped public perception and discourse about US-Israel relations. Propaganda efforts and strategic messaging aimed at portraying Israel as a steadfast ally in the fight against Soviet influence played a crucial role in garnering domestic support for pro-Israel policies. The narrative of a shared struggle against a common enemy deeply resonated with the American public, influencing the debate surrounding foreign policy decisions.

The legacy of Cold War alliances would subsequently continue to exert a significant influence on contemporary US-Israel relations. The economic and geopolitical interests that initially cemented the alliance evolved and adapted to the changing dynamics of the Middle East. This legacy serves as a reminder of the enduring nature of international strategic partnerships and the complex interplay of economic, military, and ideological factors that define them.

6
The Creation of AIPAC and Modern Zionist Lobbying
Organisation, Money and Influence

The roots of influence: historical context and origins

To understand the formation and impact of influential lobbying efforts in the United States, particularly those focused on Israel, it is essential to delve into the historical context that paved the way for these developments. Early Zionist lobbying efforts emerged in the post-war period, a time characterised by geopolitical realignments and the onset of the Cold War. The creation of the State of Israel in 1948, amid ongoing regional tensions, paved the way for concerted efforts to secure major world powers' support for the new nation. Simultaneously, the United States was emerging as a superpower, solidifying its role as a significant actor in international affairs.

The convergence of strategic interests and ideological affinities in this context laid the foundation for the influence of pro-Israel lobbying in American politics. Shared interests in expansionism, neo-colonial hegemony and hostility towards the left and Arab-Muslim nationalism, combined with funding and resources from passionate supporters, contributed to the beginnings of what would become a significant force in shaping American foreign policy.

Furthermore, the post-war economic boom in the United States provided lobbyists with the opportunity to leverage financial contributions to gain access to, and influence, decision-making processes. This intersection of economic power and political influence paved the way for the emergence of AIPAC and other organisations dedicated to promoting Israel's interests in Washington. The deepening ties between the United States and Israel, fostered by mutual defence agreements and strategic military cooperation, further strengthened their relationship and emphasised the importance of lobbying efforts to align US policies with Israel's long-term objectives as the world underwent rapid change in the second half of the 20th century, the influence of money, combined with geopolitical imperatives and ideological alignments, played a decisive role in shaping the landscape of US-Israeli relations and the associated lobbying dynamics.

Foundation of AIPAC: strategies of the early Zionist lobbies

In the aftermath of World War II, the international political landscape underwent a significant upheaval. As the United States emerged as a global superpower, its foreign policy began to exert a profound influence on the geopolitical chessboard. During this period of transformation, the young state of Israel found itself embroiled in a delicate power struggle, seeking to consolidate its position in a turbulent regional context and under the watchful eye of the international community. Central to Israel's strategic manoeuvring was the launch of targeted lobbying efforts to harness the political power of the United States.

The early days of the American Israel Public Affairs Committee (AIPAC) were characterised by clever strategies and meticulous planning to consolidate ties with key decision-makers and influencers in the American political sphere. AIPAC's strategies were multifaceted, including the establishment of extensive support networks that spanned government institutions, think tanks, and media platforms. By drawing on the rhetoric of 'shared democratic values' (Israel is the only democracy in the Middle East) and historical alliances, AIPAC has skilfully established itself as a key player in shaping American foreign policy in the Middle East.

It is important to recognise the financial support that underpins AIPAC's activities. Financial contributions from wealthy individuals, corporations, and influential donors have fuelled the organisation's activities, enabling it to accumulate considerable resources for its lobbying efforts. Through the strategic allocation of funds and the judicious use of campaign financing mechanisms, AIPAC has cemented its presence in the corridors of power, influencing policies and legislation that are important not only to Israel but also to broader regional dynamics.

Moreover, AIPAC's initial Zionist lobbying was underpinned by a nuanced understanding of economic imperatives and geopolitical alignments. It aligned itself strategically with sectors and industries that influence crucial components of the American economy and national security apparatus. By articulating narratives that resonated with American strategic interests and framing issues in terms of bilateral cooperation, AIPAC skilfully positioned itself as a vehicle for advancing the closely linked agendas of economic prosperity and geopolitical stability.

Examining the historical evolution of AIPAC's influence reveals that the strategies employed during the organisation's formative years laid the foundation for its legacy of political acumen and manoeuvrability. Early Zionist lobbying efforts set a precedent for future engagements, exemplifying the enduring symbiosis between financial clout, strategic positioning and the complex web of special interests interwoven into policymaking.

Financial power: sources of funding and contributions to election campaigns

The financial power wielded by AIPAC and other pro-Israel lobbying organisations is a key aspect of their influence on American politics. Funding flows from various sources, including wealthy donors, local supporters, and affiliated political action committees (PACs). This enables these groups to make substantial contributions to elections and support candidates who share their pro-Israel agenda. This financial leverage translates into considerable access and influence within the political establishment, enabling AIPAC to shape discourse and decision-making processes related to Middle East policy. The deep-rooted economic and geopolitical interests underlying this financial power cannot be underestimated. Israel's strategic importance in the oil-rich and geopolitically unstable Middle East region has long motivated American policymakers.

Furthermore, the American military-industrial complex has a vested interest in maintaining close ties with Israel. This opens up lucrative opportunities for arms sales and defence collaboration. Moreover, the economic and strategic alliances between Israel and the United States form part of broader geopolitical objectives, such as countering regional adversaries and exerting influence in the Middle East. The substantial financial resources available to pro-Israel lobby groups enable them to strengthen these ties and promote policies that serve Israeli and American interests. The financial clout of these lobbying entities also allows them to counter any opposition or dissenting voices within the political sphere by providing targeted financial support to their allies and coordinating efforts to marginalise their detractors. Overall, the pervasive influence of money on US foreign policy towards Israel illustrates the complex interplay between economic, geopolitical, and strategic motivations that underlie the dynamics of international relations and policymaking.

Grassroots mobilisation: popular efforts and advocacy tactics

Grassroots efforts are a crucial element of AIPAC's influence on American political institutions. By engaging with local communities and fostering ties with grassroots organisations, AIPAC has successfully mobilised a base of supporters who passionately advocate for policies aligned with Zionist interests. Through public meetings, educational seminars, and community events, AIPAC cultivates a network of individuals who can effectively convey its message to their elected representatives. This strategy harnesses the power of local voices, amplifying AIPAC's influence in policymaking. AIPAC's local advocacy tactics encompass a wide range of activities, including letter-writing, telephone campaigns, organising rallies, and petitions. These initiatives demonstrate widespread support for pro-Israel initiatives within various constituencies, pressuring policymakers to align with AIPAC's agenda.

AIPAC's substantial financial resources further strengthen

its ability to mobilise its supporters, enabling the organisation to fund targeted advertising campaigns, sponsor outreach events, and provide logistical support to local activists. Deeply rooted economic and geopolitical interests underpin these efforts. Consequently, aligning US policies with Israel's objectives strengthens strategic alliances and advances mutual defence agreements. Furthermore, the arms trade between the US and Israel highlights the economic aspect of this relationship, which plays a pivotal role in policymaking. Leveraging these closely intertwined economic and geopolitical factors, AIPAC deploys grassroots mobilisation and advocacy tactics strategically to influence policy direction, ensuring that pro-Israel perspectives remain prominent in the corridors of power.

Building alliances: engaging with American political institutions

A key aspect of AIPAC's influence lies in its skilful engagement with American political institutions. Through strategic alliances and partnerships, AIPAC has established a network of influence that reaches Congress, the White House, and other key government agencies. This complex network facilitates the promotion of policies that align with Israeli interests, often leveraging economic and geopolitical considerations to garner support. By cultivating relationships with influential legislators and administrative officials, AIPAC has effectively navigated the corridors of power in Washington. These alliances are underpinned by a complex interplay of interests, reflecting the deep-rooted links between economic incentives and foreign policy decision-making. AIPAC's ability to mobilise financial resources and direct them towards favourable candidates highlights the significant impact of money on political outcomes.

This financial leverage influences not only election campaigns but also policy-making, as elected representatives are sensitive to the preferences of well-funded interest groups. Furthermore, AIPAC's engagement with American political institutions is underpinned by a deep understanding of geopolitical dynamics. The organisation skilfully aligns its advocacy with broader American strategic objectives, particularly in the Middle East.

By framing its positions within the context of regional stability and national security, AIPAC secures bipartisan support for its policy priorities, illustrating the interconnection of economic and geopolitical interests in shaping legislative and executive actions. The multifaceted nature of these alliances is evident throughout the legislative process, where AIPAC's influence is seen in the introduction and promotion of pro-Israel bills and in preventing initiatives that are considered harmful to its interests. These concerted efforts highlight the depth of AIPAC's influence within American political institutions and demonstrate how economic incentives and geopolitical calculations combine to shape political outcomes.

As we delve deeper into this complex web of relationships, it becomes clear that the fusion of economic imperatives and geopolitical manoeuvring is the foundation of AIPAC's enduring influence within American political institutions. Understanding the nuanced interactions between monetary power and strategic interests is essential to grasping how lobbying organisations can influence domestic and foreign policy. This ultimately highlights the inherent complexity of the relationship between money, politics and national interests.

Media and communication: controlling the narrative

In the context of political influence and lobbying, shaping the narrative is a critical aspect of orchestrating political change. AIPAC and modern Zionist lobbying groups recognise the immense power that controlling the media and messaging confers in influencing public opinion and ultimately policymakers. Through clever communication strategies and skilful use of various media platforms, these groups can effectively shape the discourse around Israel and Middle Eastern policies, thereby influencing public opinion and government actions.

Financial support from influential donors enables these lobbying organisations to access and influence the media through advertising, sponsored content and direct communication with journalists and editors. By framing issues strategically, these groups can steer public debate in line with their geopolitical and economic interests. Moreover, their ability to control discourse extends beyond traditional media to social media and digital spaces, where carefully crafted messages can quickly permeate public consciousness. Furthermore, the symbiotic relationship between pro-Israel lobbies and the media affects news presentation and information dissemination.

By emphasising certain aspects of events while downplaying others, these lobbying groups can negatively influence public perception of complex geopolitical situations. Propagating favourable narratives serves not only to garner domestic support but also to influence international opinion, thereby protecting crucial foreign policy decisions. The framing of debates and discussions concerning Israel and the Middle East also plays a decisive role in virtually all important political decisions.

By disseminating persuasive discourse and tailored narratives, these pressure groups construct the framework through which policymakers perceive key issues, ensuring their economic and geopolitical interests remain at the forefront of decision-making processes. This strategic manipulation of the media landscape reinforces the pervasive influence of well-funded lobbying efforts on policy direction and outcomes.

Case studies: landmark legislation and policy changes

Throughout history, AIPAC and other pro-Israel lobby groups have played a significant role in influencing major legislative and policy changes within the US government. One notable example is the passage of the US-Israel Enhanced Security Cooperation Act in 2012. This legislation reaffirmed the unbreakable bond between the US and Israel and committed the US to providing Israel with the military capabilities necessary to maintain its qualitative military edge in the region. The influence of lobbying efforts, strategic alliances and financial contributions in the passage of such crucial legislation cannot be underestimated.

Another decisive example is the assistance provided to Israel through foreign aid programmes. As the United States is the largest donor of military aid to Israel, the lobbying power wielded by groups such as AIPAC has been crucial in maintaining support for these programmes. The underlying economic interests are manifold and include promoting the US defence industry, maintaining regional stability and securing geopolitical influence in the Middle East.

Furthermore, the transfer of the US Embassy from Tel Aviv to Jerusalem is a particularly striking case when examining policy changes. Despite long-standing international norms and diplomatic protocols, the embassy's relocation emphasised the strength of lobbying efforts and the geopolitical interests at stake. This decision symbolises a broader alignment with Israeli positions. It signals a shift in the US's approach to the Israeli–Palestinian conflict, reflecting the influence of powerful lobbying and deeply rooted economic and strategic motivations.

These case studies highlight the complex interplay of money, influence and deep-seated motivations underlying American policy decisions regarding Israel. The intricate web of economic and geopolitical interests, coupled with the formidable lobbying power of organisations such as AIPAC, continues to shape significant legislative milestones and policy shifts in US–Israel relations.

Economic interests: arms trade and mutual defence

The economic interests underlying the arms trade and mutual defence agreements between the United States and Israel have played a decisive role in shaping foreign policy decisions. For decades, the United States has been a major supplier of advanced military equipment and technology to Israel, with annual aid programmes amounting to billions of dollars. These substantial arms transfers not only strengthen Israel's security but also boost the US defence industry, fostering a symbiotic relationship that blends national security imperatives with economic considerations. Furthermore, the arms trade forms the basis of a strategic alliance, cementing the interdependence and cooperation between the two nations, extending beyond immediate financial transactions.

This collaboration extends to intelligence sharing, joint military exercises and defence research and development initiatives, as well as conventional weapons systems. The supply of sophisticated weapons to Israel is strategically linked to US geopolitical objectives in the Middle East, thereby strengthening its influence and presence in an unstable region. Moreover, mutual defence agreements between the US and Israel act as a deterrent and stabilising force against shared regional adversaries, thereby safeguarding US interests and allies.

The strategic positioning of Israeli military capabilities aligns with broader US security strategies, enabling Washington to project its power and influence in a turbulent Middle East. Understanding the deep intertwining of economic and geopolitical complexities within these defence agreements is essential. Injecting funds into the US defence sector boosts domestic production, technological innovation, and skilled employment opportunities. From a geopolitical perspective, these arms transfers and mutual defence pacts simultaneously underpin the alignment of interests in combating common regional threats and provide the United States with a key ally in advancing its broader strategic objectives. While economic interests are evident, they form part of a complex interaction with broader geopolitical considerations and regional dynamics. The exchange of military equipment illustrates the fusion of defence needs and economic benefits, shaping political outcomes at national and international levels. Elucidating the multifaceted nature of foreign policy decision-making requires an understanding of the complex links between economic incentives, security imperatives and geopolitical interdependencies.

Geopolitical Calculations: Alignments in Middle East Politics

Within the complex web of international relations, geopolitics has long played a central role in shaping alliances and conflicts in the Middle East. To grasp these dynamics, it is crucial to recognise the influence of economic and strategic interests underlying political decisions. The most significant of these are the intricate relationships between various regional powers and how their objectives align with those of influential pressure groups, such as AIPAC. The interplay of economic incentives, security agreements and political manoeuvring offers a valuable perspective through which to analyse the ever-changing landscape of Middle Eastern politics.

At the heart of geopolitical calculations in the region lies the quest for dominance and influence. States compete for a strategic advantage to secure access to vital resources, protect their national security, and expand their sphere of influence. These objectives often intertwine with the broader agendas of global powers, adding multiple layers of complexity to the geopolitical chessboard. The alignment of these objectives, whether overt or covert, shapes the policies and alliances that emerge on the regional stage. Furthermore, the intersection of economic drivers and geopolitical imperatives highlights the intricate power dynamics in the Middle East. Economic partnerships, energy dependencies and trade relations are intertwined with strategic alliances and military cooperation, creating a delicate ecosystem of interdependence.

This interconnectedness influences political decisions and catalyses establishing long-term geopolitical alignments. Examining the historical evolution of politics in the Middle East more closely reveals the enduring importance of geopolitical calculations. From Cold War rivalries to contemporary struggles for hegemony, the region has been the setting for a battle between competing interests and ideologies.

Today, the context of geopolitical realignments continues to influence diplomatic relations and military interventions. The convergence of economic imperatives, military strategies and ideological affiliations reflects the ongoing power play that characterises Middle Eastern politics. As we unravel the complex web of geopolitical calculations, it becomes clear that the intersection of money, power and influence has a profound impact on policy formulation and execution in the Middle East. Understanding these deeply rooted dynamics is essential to grasping the forces that shape the region's trajectory, as well as to critically assessing the implications of geopolitical manoeuvring for regional stability and international relations.

Criticism and counter-movements: challenges to AIPAC's dominance

The American Israel Public Affairs Committee (AIPAC)'s influence on US policy towards the Middle East has not gone unnoticed and has faced criticism and opposition. As the most powerful pro-Israel lobby group, AIPAC has faced challenges from various quarters due to its perceived dominance in influencing US foreign policy. Critics have expressed concerns about AIPAC's disproportionate influence on US policy decisions relating to the Middle East, alleging that it hinders the pursuit of a balanced approach to the region's complex dynamics. Furthermore, there have been debates regarding the impact of financial contributions from AIPAC and its supporters on the US government's decision-making process, raising questions about the extent to which money influences policy outcomes.

Counter-movements have also emerged, advocating a re-evaluation of US support for Israel and promoting alternative solutions to the Israeli-Palestinian conflict. These efforts aim to challenge AIPAC's influence and encourage a more nuanced and inclusive approach to policymaking in the region. Economic considerations also play an important role in scrutinising AIPAC's dominance, with critics highlighting the numerous economic interests tied to US–Israel relations. Given the substantial military aid and trade agreements between the two countries, concerns have been raised about the effect of these agreements on broader geopolitical and economic considerations.

Moreover, geopolitical alliances and security commitments are under scrutiny, particularly regarding the implications of unreserved support for Israel for regional stability and US global interests. The evolving landscape of international relations and changing dynamics in the Middle East have prompted closer scrutiny of AIPAC's strategies and objectives, fuelling discussions about the need for an inclusive approach and diplomatic balance in shaping US policy.

Initiatives that seek to amplify the diversity of voices and perspectives within the American political sphere aim to counterbalance AIPAC's perceived singular influence. The goal is to foster a more comprehensive and informed approach to the complexities of the Middle East region. As the debate over AIPAC's dominance continues to evolve, it is evident that the organisation's influence extends across various aspects of global politics, economics, and security. This has prompted critical evaluations and efforts to adjust the dynamics of US involvement in the Middle East.

7
From Capitol Hill to the White House
How Lobbying Has Reshaped American Politics

The Origins of Lobbying Power: A Historical Overview

Throughout the history of the United States, lobbying has played a significant role in shaping political decisions and policies. The practice has evolved since the nation's early days, when influential individuals and groups sought to influence government actions.

Initially, lobbying was conducted informally, with wealthy elites using personal connections and financial incentives to influence decision-makers. However, as the country grew and industrialisation took hold, lobbying began to formalise and expand. Industries such as railways, oil, and banking emerged as influential lobbying players, leveraging their economic weight to advance their interests. This marked a shift towards corporate lobbying, where financial power became synonymous with political influence.

As economic disparities widened, lobbying also became a means for marginalised groups to defend their rights and interests. The civil rights movement, trade unions, and environmental activists all employed lobbying to advocate for social and legislative change. Over time, lobbying evolved from merely defending a cause to becoming a sophisticated, well-funded industry that permeates all levels of government.

The fusion of wealth, corporate power and geopolitical interests has created a complex network of influence that continues to shape political decisions. The concentration of economic power in specific industries has enabled the consolidation of political influence and the promotion of policies that serve their interests. Furthermore, the intertwining of economic and geopolitical ambitions has helped to project American influence abroad.

Lobbying relating to defence contracts, international trade agreements and the allocation of foreign aid illustrates how money and power exert influence beyond national borders. Consequently, an overview of the historical development of lobbying power not only reveals its origins in early American society but also its evolution into an omnipresent force that influences domestic and foreign policy decisions. The implications of this evolution are considerable, impacting the democratic process, socio-economic equality and global stability.

Building alliances: key players and funders

The network of power and influence extends far beyond the halls of Capitol Hill, encompassing a web of key players and funders closely linked to the political decision-making process. At the heart of this complex network are influential individuals and organisations whose substantial financial contributions shape policy in line with their particular interests.

Large corporations, wealthy donors and special interest groups converge in this context to consolidate their position as influential players in the corridors of power. They cultivate their alliances through strategic patronage, maintaining symbiotic relationships with policymakers who can advance their agendas. These entities' considerable financial resources ensure them access to decision-makers, granting them a powerful voice in shaping laws and regulations that align with their economic objectives. Furthermore, geopolitical interests intertwine with economic imperatives, amplifying the stakes and complexities inherent in lobbying efforts.

As international dynamics come into play, global entities seek to protect and promote their strategic objectives by leveraging their financial influence in Washington. By forming alliances with policymakers who are sensitive to geopolitical considerations, these entities aim to further their broader agendas and influence the direction of U.S. foreign policy.

Consequently, the convergence of economic and geopolitical interests underpins the pervasive influence wielded by key players and funders, enabling them to reshape US policies to their advantage. This complex interaction highlights the ongoing influence of money, alliances and diverse interests in shaping the complexities of US governance.

Access and influence: electoral contributions as a means of pressure

We cannot ignore the important role that electoral contributions play in influencing political decisions. The power of money in politics extends beyond mere financial transactions; it serves as a means of exerting pressure, opening doors to policymakers and influencing their decisions in favour of particular interests. Campaign contributions enable individuals and organisations to access and influence the political sphere, thereby shaping policy direction.

However, this practice raises crucial questions about the integrity and independence of decision-making in democratic systems. These contributions are often motivated by deep-rooted economic and geopolitical interests, reflecting the pursuit of policies that favour particular agendas.

Large corporations, for example, may strategically allocate funds to political campaigns in anticipation of regulatory or legislative outcomes that favour their business objectives. Similarly, foreign entities may seek to influence American policy to serve their geopolitical ambitions by providing financial support to candidates who are sympathetic to their cause. The close relationship between campaign contributions and policy outcomes underscores the intricate interplay between financial incentives and governance. Furthermore, the influx of financial resources into political campaigns raises concerns about the disproportionate influence of wealth on the democratic process. In such circumstances, can we still speak of representative democracy? Moreover, if so, who is represented: the ordinary people or the wealthy? The common people or the wealthy? If it were the wealthy, it would be more of an oligarchy than a true democracy. Nevertheless, let us not stray from our subject.

As this dynamic continues to evolve, it is crucial to examine the relationship between election campaign contributions and political decisions in order to uphold the principles of democratic representation and public interest. Recognising the complex network of economic and geopolitical factors underlying electoral contributions is essential to grasping their profound implications for national and international political landscapes.

Beyond cheques: the promise of economic benefits

The promise of economic benefits is a seductive force in American policy development influenced by lobbying. Beyond campaign donations and political contributions, lobbyists emphasise the potential economic gains that could result from aligning with specific foreign interests or entities. This appeal extends beyond immediate financial gains to encompass long-term economic partnerships, trade agreements and market access. Sometimes, the economic incentives presented by lobbyists are intertwined with broader geopolitical strategies.

The desire to strengthen ties with certain countries or regions may be motivated by the acquisition of resources, the expansion of markets for American companies, or the positioning of the United States strategically within global economic networks. These promises are particularly compelling when presented in the context of national economic growth, job creation and strengthening US competitiveness in global markets. The subtleties of the economic benefits promised by lobbying efforts are often woven into narratives touting mutual benefits, emphasising how aligning US policy with the interests of lobbying entities would yield reciprocal gains for the nation and its stakeholders. These narratives are carefully constructed to highlight the perceived benefits while downplaying the potential risks or implications for other sectors of society.

However, these promises conceal complex power dynamics and special interests that extend far beyond simple financial considerations. The interaction between economic benefits and policymaking has significant implications for international relations and global power structures. It can shape alliances, influence trade patterns and determine resource allocation, thereby perpetuating a cycle of influence and reinforcing the interdependence of economic and geopolitical forces. As we delve deeper into this complex web of economic incentives and their role in shaping policy, it becomes clear that the lure of economic benefits, when leveraged through lobbying channels, has the potential to alter the course of American diplomacy and global engagement fundamentally. Understanding these motivations in depth reveals the intricate relationship between economic interests and political decisions, and highlights the complexities underlying modern policymaking.

Geopolitical dynamics: interests that transcend oceans

Throughout history, nations have sought to expand their power and influence globally, often driven by economic and geopolitical interests that transcend national borders. The interaction between these factors has often shaped international policies and alliances, creating a complex web of relationships that impact global dynamics. At the heart of this web lies money's immense power to steer the course of diplomacy and politics far beyond national capitals. Geopolitical interests, fuelled by economic imperatives, drive nations to seek strategic advantages in distant lands. This often involves forming alliances with countries that possess valuable resources or crucial geographical positions. These alliances are influenced not only by the pursuit of economic opportunities but also by the desire to counterbalance the influence of rival powers. Through strategic investments and trade agreements, nations seek to secure access to vital resources while projecting their influence in different regions. The political dimensions of these agreements are equally important, reflecting the intertwining of economic and geopolitical objectives. Leveraging their financial clout, lobbyists and corporations play a central role in shaping the situation by channelling their influence to align policies with their particular interests.

The intersection of economic incentives and geopolitical strategy can fuel intense competition between nations, resulting in diplomatic manoeuvring to secure advantageous positions on the global stage. This can manifest as territorial disputes or attempts to establish a military presence in strategic locations. As policymakers navigate these complexities, they must carefully consider the economic and geopolitical implications of their decisions, weighing up the immediate benefits against the long-term consequences for their nation's position on the international stage. The intersection of financial interests and strategic objectives often gives rise to intricate geopolitical manoeuvres that reverberate across continents, impacting global stability and shaping the course of international relations. Understanding the intricate relationship between economic and geopolitical motivations provides policymakers with insight into the underlying dynamics that determine the course of world affairs.

Political Machines: Mechanisms of Political Persuasion

Political entities in the United States have a wide range of mechanisms at their disposal to shape and influence policy. At the heart of these 'machines' lies a complex network of relationships, financial incentives, and strategic manoeuvres that function as levers of persuasion in the corridors of power. Lobbying firms, corporate interests, and other influential groups utilise their substantial financial resources to gain access to decision-makers and politicians, thereby positioning themselves at the centre of political influence. The interaction between capital and control shapes the direction of national policies by converging economic and geopolitical interests. The prospect of lucrative commercial transactions, trade agreements, and international alliances further accentuates the grip these machines have on policy formulation and implementation. The intricate relationship between financial powers and political figures is often obscured from public view, perpetuating the perception that decisions are insulated from special interests.

However, the truth is that these machines are integral to political persuasion, using their financial weight to manipulate political outcomes in line with their own objectives. Deeply rooted alliances and patronage networks exert considerable influence by blurring the lines between governance and the special interests that guide it. This political persuasion machine not only operates on home soil but also extends its influence across oceans. It leverages economic and geopolitical incentives to shape international relations in a manner that aligns with the agendas of a privileged few. Therefore, it is essential to comprehend the inner workings of these political mechanisms to grasp the complexities of modern diplomacy and international cooperation, and to shed light on the clandestine forces that shape governance. Within the complex mechanisms of political persuasion, economic power and geopolitical strategy converge to shape the destiny of nations and the world order as a whole.

Lobbying in action: case studies of political change

Throughout history, the influence of lobbying on political decisions has been undeniable. The intersection of economic and geopolitical interests with political power has frequently resulted in substantial shifts in governmental priorities, both domestically and internationally. To understand this impact, we examine a series of case studies that illustrate the profound influence of lobbying. One such case study concerns environmental policy.

Powerful lobbying efforts by the fossil fuel industry have led to intense opposition to emissions regulations and environmental protection, resulting in the relaxation of standards and a significant shift away from eco-centric policies. This phenomenon reflects the strong influence of financial interests on environmental legislation, despite its critical importance to public health and ecological sustainability. Another compelling case study concerns the arms trade sector. Lobbying by defence contractors and their subsidiaries has consistently promoted policies favouring increased military spending and expansive defence contracts. Geopolitical motivations intertwine with economic gains as policy decisions align with the lucrative goals of these influential entities, often at the expense of peacebuilding initiatives and international security collaboration.

Furthermore, the healthcare sector is a striking example of the impact of lobbying on policy development. Pharmaceutical companies, insurance conglomerates, and medical institutions have considerable influence, perpetuating a system that prioritises profitability over access to affordable healthcare. This alignment of financial incentives with political power profoundly shapes the landscape of health policy, hindering progress towards universal coverage and the equitable delivery of medical services. The technology sector also provides a relevant case study. Lobbying efforts by tech giants have considerably influenced privacy regulations, antitrust measures, and intellectual property laws. The fusion of financial power and strategic lobbying has led to policies that reflect the tech sector's preferences, often overlooking broader considerations such as consumer rights and fair competition.

In summary, these case studies highlight the significant impact of lobbying on policy change, where the interaction between money, economic agendas, and geopolitical objectives has a considerable influence on legislative decisions. Understanding these dynamics is therefore essential for discerning the forces that drive governance and the complex network of relationships that underpin policymaking.

Resistance and compliance: navigating the waters of Congress

The complex process of policymaking in the United States often involves negotiating the turbulent waters of Congress. As lobbyists seek to advance their agendas, they encounter a variety of responses from legislators, creating a complex landscape of resistance and compliance, driven by diverse interests. At the heart of this dynamic is the power of money and its influence on decisions made within these hallowed chambers.

When confronted with lobbying efforts, members of Congress must carefully consider competing demands from their constituents, their partisan affiliations and their personal convictions. This delicate balancing act often results in resistance to specific policy proposals, particularly when they contradict popular opinion. However, the persuasive power of financial support from special interest groups and corporations can pose a significant challenge to this resistance. Furthermore, geopolitical and economic interests further complicate Congress's decision-making landscape. Global alliances, trade agreements, and strategic partnerships all play a crucial role in shaping legislators' positions. The allure of economic opportunities and the pressures of international diplomacy can lead to instances of surprising conformity, even in the face of initial opposition.

To shed light on the behind-the-scenes negotiations that determine the direction of national policy, it is essential to meticulously analyse the nuanced interactions between lobbyists and members of Congress. Through in-depth research and detailed case studies, we can begin to understand the complex web of incentives and pressures at play in legislative processes, revealing the intricate relationship between resistance, compliance and the quest for accurate representation in a democracy.

Presidential politics: from advisers to Oval Office decisions

Presidential politics in the United States is a complex web of competing interests, ideologies and influences. The influence of money and lobbying on presidential decisions is significant. Advisers play a central role in shaping a president's worldview and policies. However, the influence of economic and geopolitical interests on political decisions is significant. Lobbying efforts target not only elected officials but also their advisers, to shape their views on key issues.

Lobbyists and wealthy donors enjoy proximity to power, enabling them to advocate directly for their interests to those who influence the president's decisions. This creates an environment in which policy decisions can be influenced by factors such as financial support, strategic alliances and the promise of economic benefits. Economic and geopolitical interests often intertwine with political decisions, with pressure to prioritise these concerns increasingly influencing presidential actions.

The Oval Office itself becomes the centre of intense lobbying efforts, with various interests seeking to influence the president's agenda directly. Understanding the interaction between financial interests and decisions made at the highest levels of government is essential. Recognising this reality enables us better to understand the deeper motivations behind many policy choices. Looking to the future, it is clear that understanding how lobbying influences presidential policy is crucial for comprehending the trajectory of American diplomacy and governance.

Future Outlook: The Future of Lobbying-Influenced Diplomacy

To envision the future of lobbying-influenced diplomacy, it is necessary to critically analyse the current dynamics shaping American foreign policy and anticipate how these will evolve. The influence exerted by lobbying entities has become an integral part of diplomatic decision-making, often closely linked to economic and geopolitical imperatives. In the future, the connection between money, interests, and political orientation is likely to strengthen, posing a challenge to the concept of impartial, principle-based governance.

A key trend on the horizon is the growing sophistication and diversification of the tactics used by lobbying groups to advocate for their interests. With advanced technologies and data analytics at their disposal, these entities can refine their approaches, thereby strengthening their influence on policymaking. Furthermore, as global interdependencies and economic alliances become more complex, the convergence of national and international interests will result in greater focus on lobbying efforts. Policies that serve national interests and align with the objectives of influential allies will profoundly shape the diplomatic landscape. Additionally, the emergence of new economic powers and the resurgence of historical geopolitical actors will reshape the contours of lobbying influence. As these entities expand their influence across various regions, their ability to shape political paradigms will have a profound impact on international relations, affecting the balance of power and the trajectory of global developments.

Another noteworthy development is the evolution of the legal and regulatory framework surrounding lobbying activities. Stricter regulations could be adopted to limit undue influence and promote transparency. Conversely, relaxing restrictions encourage pressure groups to intensify their efforts. The interaction between legal constraints and the fluid nature of lobbying tactics will undoubtedly influence future diplomatic arenas.

However, amid these projections, there is a glimmer of hope for rebalancing. Growing awareness of the harmful consequences of unchecked lobbying power provides an opportunity for civic engagement and the promotion of systemic reforms. Movements calling for ethical governance and equitable representation have the power to create waves of change, pushing back against the tide of disproportionate influence. Furthermore, as public scrutiny intensifies and information becomes more accessible, democratic principles may become more resilient, fostering adjustments in the relationship between lobbying and diplomacy. Reassessing the balance between private interests and the public good is a pivotal moment in the future of lobbying-driven diplomacy. As this paradigm continues to evolve, vigilance, critical thinking, and concerted efforts towards institutional integrity will be essential in steering diplomatic discourse towards a more equitable and ethical trajectory.

8
Silencing Debate
Media Narratives and the Cost of Dissent in Washington

The Anatomy of Influence: The Media as Policymakers

The media plays a central role in shaping public opinion and influencing political decisions. The interaction between money, economic interests, and geopolitical agendas has created a complex web of influence within the media landscape. Contributions to election campaigns and editorial bias significantly influence the shaping of media narratives to align with specific political and commercial interests. The injection of money into the media often leads to subtle or overt editorial bias that favours certain viewpoints while marginalising others.

Economic and geopolitical interests wield considerable power behind the scenes in determining which topics will be highlighted and how they will be presented. Think tanks and wealthy donors fund the media, shaping the discourse on crucial issues such as foreign policy, trade agreements and national security. The media often rely on experts affiliated with these entities, thereby amplifying their views and embedding certain political positions in the public consciousness. This process extends beyond simple news reporting into opinion pieces and editorial content. These platforms are used to articulate and promote specific political objectives that are often aligned with the economic and geopolitical interests of their funders.

Consequently, the public is presented with a biased version of reality that favours the interests of powerful actors rather than providing an impartial view of the world. Furthermore, the way the media presents conflicts and crises often reflects the broader geopolitical strategies of these influential actors. Issues are contextualised in a way that corresponds to specific foreign policy objectives, thereby reinforcing existing power structures rather than challenging them.

Consequently, media representations of international events can be manipulated to validate particular interests, perpetuating a status quo that favours dominant powers. In light of these dynamics, it is crucial to critically evaluate the media's role in shaping public discourse and influencing political outcomes. Understanding the complex relationships between money, economic interests, and geopolitical agendas helps uncover the underlying motivations driving media narratives, thereby achieving a more transparent and accountable media landscape.

Money talks: election campaign contributions and editorial bias

The intersection of money, politics, and the media creates a complex web of influences that shapes public opinion and political decisions. Contributions to election campaigns from wealthy individuals, corporations and interest groups often come with the implicit expectation of favourable treatment, creating a system in which financial influence can sway political outcomes. Deep-rooted economic and geopolitical interests significantly influence these contributions, as donors seek to advance their agendas and protect their assets, both domestically and internationally. Motivations behind these financial investments in politics include resource allocation, market access, and the pursuit of strategic alliances.

This dynamic of intertwined money and power also extends to the editorial decisions of major media outlets. Whether subtle or overt, editorial biases can significantly influence the narratives presented to the public, thereby shaping public discourse and ultimately policy direction. Journalists and media outlets may find themselves under pressure to align their coverage with the preferences of their benefactors, consciously or unconsciously shaping their reporting so as not to 'bite the hand that feeds them'. Consequently, critical voices that challenge the status quo or advocate policies contrary to the interests of major donors are often marginalised or excluded from mainstream platforms, perpetuating a cycle of limited viewpoint diversity.

This financial influence distorts democratic principles by overshadowing the voice of the electorate with the amplified megaphones of influential donors. Economic disparities in political participation lead to biased representation, creating an environment in which special interests often take precedence over the public interest. Ultimately, the interplay between monetary influence and editorial control undermines the fundamental principles of democracy, fostering an environment in which political decisions are influenced by wealthy individuals rather than the collective well-being of society. Understanding and confronting these dynamics is essential to preserving the integrity of democratic processes and promoting policies that genuinely serve the interests of the people.

Think tanks and media experts: shaping the discourse

Think tanks and experts play a central role in shaping public opinion and political discourse. These entities wield considerable influence through their ability to craft narratives that align with particular economic and geopolitical interests. Often funded by corporations and interest groups, think tanks produce research and analysis that can influence public opinion and inform government decisions. Through strategic media positioning, they disseminate their views to the general public. This amplification is further reinforced by the participation of 'commentators', eloquent individuals who frequently appear on news programmes to present expert views. While these individuals may appear impartial, their connections to particular organisations or agendas can subtly skew the discourse in favour of those with financial interests in specific policy outcomes.

The symbiotic relationship between think tanks and the media also influences the topics that feature prominently in the news cycle. By influencing the media agenda, these entities can draw attention to issues that benefit their funders while diverting attention away from topics that might challenge existing power structures or contradict established narratives. Furthermore, the language used by think tanks and experts is carefully constructed to frame debates in a way that favours their benefactors.

This strategic use of language can influence public understanding of complex issues, effectively steering interpretations in a direction that serves specific interests. Thus, the framing of discourse by think tanks and commentators influences public opinion and shapes political discussions and decisions. The implications extend beyond the mere dissemination of information to actively guiding the course of governance. Recognising this reality is essential to understanding the deep forces at work in the political landscape, where economic and geopolitical interests intertwine with media manoeuvring to exert considerable influence on policymaking.

Setting the agenda: how news priorities are chosen

In modern democratic societies, the media plays a crucial role in shaping public opinion and influencing political discourse. However, the process of selecting news priorities is often opaque and influenced by various factors, including economic and geopolitical interests. Although news organisations claim to prioritise objectivity and the public interest, the reality is often different, with agendas being set according to the preferences of powerful interest groups and advertisers. The interaction between money and influence must be considered when analysing how news priorities are determined. Large corporations and wealthy individuals can influence media coverage through advertising revenue, sponsorship deals and direct media ownership. This can directly impact the types of stories covered and how they are approached. Economic and geopolitical interests also play an important role in shaping media agendas.

News organisations may prioritise topics that align with the economic interests of their owners or sponsors while considering the potential geopolitical ramifications of their coverage. For instance, international events may be covered in a manner that aligns with a government's foreign policy objectives or the interests of its key allies. Additionally, media priorities are determined by the perceived needs and preferences of the public.

Media outlets often rely on market research and audience feedback to identify topics that will attract the largest audience. This can result in a focus on sensational or entertaining content at the expense of more substantial issues. Furthermore, the 24-hour news cycle and the rise of digital media have accelerated the pace at which news priorities are determined. The speed of media coverage and the need for attention-grabbing headlines have led to a focus on topics that immediately capture attention, to the detriment of important yet less sensational issues. Consequently, the power dynamics inherent in media prioritisation have broader implications for democratic governance and public engagement. Understanding the complex mechanisms that determine the media agenda enables us to critically examine the information presented to us and work towards a more transparent and inclusive media landscape.

Voices in the Wilderness: The Marginalisation of Dissent

In a political landscape dominated by well-established interests and powerful lobbies, dissenting voices often find themselves marginalised and silenced. This is particularly evident in media discourse, where narratives are carefully crafted to serve specific agendas. The power of money and the influence of economic and geopolitical interests play a central role in defining the limits of acceptable discourse. Those who challenge the status quo or prevailing policies encounter substantial obstacles to meaningful participation in public discourse. Their views are overshadowed by the amplification of voices that align with existing power structures.

The marginalisation of dissent has profound implications for democratic governance, reducing the scope of public discourse and undermining the diversity of viewpoints that are essential for informed decision-making. The mechanisms by which dissent is suppressed are manifold. Financial considerations often dictate media priorities, determining which voices are amplified. Institutions and individuals with vested interests use their financial resources to shape media narratives, thereby influencing the content and framing of public discourse. Furthermore, the institutionalisation of certain viewpoints through think tanks and strategic partnerships perpetuates the marginalisation of dissent.

Control processes within media organisations filter out viewpoints that deviate from dominant paradigms, thereby reinforcing homogeneity of opinion. The pervasive influence of geopolitical agendas further complicates the landscape of dissent. Critics of policies that align with strategic national interests may face concerted efforts to delegitimise their viewpoints or portray them as unpatriotic. Framing conflicts and issues in language steeped in power dynamics reinforces existing hierarchies and prevents the emergence of alternative viewpoints.

In light of these challenges, it is crucial to examine the structural inequalities within the media ecosystem that perpetuate the marginalisation of dissenting voices. To reclaim space for divergent voices, concerted efforts must be made to counter the undue influence of money and special interests in shaping media narratives.

This requires promoting transparency in media ownership, encouraging independent investigative journalism and diversifying sources of information. By recognising the power dynamics at work and actively fighting against the marginalisation of dissenting voices, we can work towards a more robust and democratic exchange of ideas. The vitality of democratic societies depends on their ability to accept and consider diverse points of view, transcending the constraints imposed by established interests.

Framing conflict: language, power and perception

Language is not only a tool for communication; it is also a weapon of influence capable of shaping perceptions and legitimising power relations. In geopolitics, the strategic use of language is key to defining conflicts and justifying political decisions. In this context, it is also necessary to analyse the complex web of linguistic manipulation that maintains the status quo and perpetuates the interests of influential individuals and groups.

The interplay between economic and geopolitical interests fuels the orchestration of linguistic narratives that bolster the existing power structure. Through their choice of words and carefully crafted rhetoric, policymakers and the media shape public opinion to align it with their agendas. For example, deliberately labelling regional conflicts as 'threats' or 'alliances' reflects a calculated effort to garner support for specific actors and initiatives. Furthermore, dehumanising or demonising certain groups through language helps justify military interventions or economic sanctions. These linguistic strategies reinforce existing power dynamics and support the interests of those with economic and geopolitical leverage. Additionally, the pervasiveness of money in politics amplifies the influence of language in shaping public discourse.

Financial support from special interest groups promotes the dissemination of favourable discourse, stifling dissenting voices and opposing viewpoints. Powerful actors with economic influence can dictate the language used in political discussions and media coverage, advancing their particular interests under the guise of objective discourse.

Moreover, the intersection of economic and geopolitical interests permeates language through indirect channels, such as think tanks and lobbying efforts. These entities craft language that presents policies favouring specific economic alliances or enterprises as being essential to national security or global stability. By presenting these policies as imperatives, their proponents seek to exploit public opinion and minimise opposition. Researchers must closely examine the manipulation of language in the dissemination of information and the formulation of policies. Recognising the subtle, yet profound impact of linguistic framing enables us to expose underlying power structures and hold them accountable for their use of language. This understanding enables us to restore the integrity of public discourse and advocate transparency in the articulation of geopolitical decisions.

Geopolitical agendas: supporting strategic allies through the media

The media plays a vital role in shaping public perceptions and attitudes towards geopolitical allies and adversaries. This influence is often leveraged to support strategic allies through carefully crafted narratives and biased media coverage, reflecting the deep economic and geopolitical interests that underpin political decisions. Behind this influential image lies a complex network of financial support, political manoeuvring and strategic messaging. At the heart of this dynamic is the flow of money from interest groups, lobbyists and foreign actors seeking to promote their own agendas and advance their national interests. These financial resources are directed towards the media, think tanks and political campaigns, thereby influencing the representation of international relations and potentially swaying public opinion. Economic ties and military alliances further amplify the impact of these narratives, highlighting the interdependent relationship between the media, money, and geopolitics.

Tactics commonly employed in this arena include conducting smear campaigns against nations considered adversaries, strategically amplifying the voices of allies, and framing conflicts in a manner that aligns with national interests. The media's power to shape public perception reinforces the strategic importance of maintaining a positive image of allies and casting doubt on the motivations and actions of adversaries. This control of discourse also extends to international crises and conflicts, where strategic allies can benefit from amplified, favourable media coverage to justify military interventions or economic partnerships that serve political and economic objectives.

Furthermore, the presentation of geopolitical events can be used to garner public support for policies that align with the interests of influential stakeholders, thus reinforcing the complex link between media influence and geopolitical agendas. The symbiotic relationship between the media and political institutions perpetuates a cycle of influence: policymakers utilise media platforms to communicate and justify their foreign policies, while the media relies on access to official sources for information and exclusives. This entanglement of interests can lead to the marginalisation or silencing of critical analyses and alternative perspectives that challenge the discourse presented by those in power. Understanding the depth of these links and their powerful influence on public perception is essential to deciphering the complexity of international relations and the media's role in promoting geopolitical agendas. By closely examining the interdependent nature of money, the media, and geopolitical interests, we can gain a deeper understanding of how strategic alliances are cultivated, defended, and promoted through media representation.

Silencing Critics: Case Studies of Journalistic Retaliation

In the complex relationship between the media and politics, cases of retaliation against critics are not uncommon. The power dynamics at work in Washington extend to the realm of journalism, where dissenting voices can be silenced and marginalised. Recent case studies reveal the chilling effect on investigative journalism and critical analysis when these fields challenge established power structures and vested interests.

Notably, investigative journalists have been subjected to intimidation and reprisals for exposing the close ties between corporate lobbyists and elected officials. They were targeted by smear campaigns and defamation attempts aimed at discrediting their work and deterring others from conducting similar investigations. Furthermore, the relationship between media conglomerates and government agencies highlights how criticising policies linked to economic and geopolitical interests can lead to swift repercussions. Journalists seeking to unravel the complexities of trade agreements, military interventions or international alliances often find themselves under pressure to alter their narratives, or risk losing access to privileged information. This insidious form of coercion underscores the subtle yet pervasive nature of the forces that stifle critical discourse. Additionally, conflicts of interest within media organisations raise concerns about compromised editorial independence and the proliferation of biased narratives. Cases in which journalists with connections to influential figures have been shielded from scrutiny emphasise the symbiotic relationship between financial interests and the media.

These examples demonstrate how financial influence can distort the presentation of factual evidence and limit the scope of public discourse. Beyond these individual cases, the broader impact of silencing critics is felt throughout society, contributing to a climate in which courageous investigative journalism is increasingly sidelined in favour of sensationalism and innocuous reporting. As economic and geopolitical interests continue to shape political discourse, the suppression of dissenting voices remains a powerful means of maintaining the status quo. Therefore, it is essential to understand the covert methods used to stifle criticism to uncover the structural barriers to transparent and accountable governance. This chapter examines patterns of journalistic reprisals and their ramifications for democratic processes, emphasising the need for renewed vigilance to preserve press freedom and foster a culture of fearless inquiry.

Public opinion and public policy: the role of the media in the divide

The relationship between public opinion and public policy is complex and often misunderstood. The media plays a central role in this dynamic, serving as a conduit for public opinion while also influencing policy decisions. At the heart of this interaction lies the considerable power wielded by economic and geopolitical interests, which can distort the alignment between public wishes and the policies implemented. This divergence is based on a complex set of factors.

Firstly, economic incentives encourage media companies to favour narratives that align with their financial interests. Advertisers and the companies that support them can pressure the media to promote content that supports their agendas, creating an environment where profit takes precedence over impartial reporting. Consequently, the information presented to the public may be filtered through a lens that prioritises commercial gain over truthful reporting, resulting in a discrepancy between public perception and the actual implications of policies. Furthermore, geopolitical interests further complicate this divide. International alliances, trade agreements and strategic partnerships influence the alignment of media discourse with government policies.

When a country's foreign policy is closely linked to economic or security agreements, the media may be incentivised to disseminate narratives that preserve diplomatic relations or serve national interests, even if these diverge from public opinion. This convergence of political and economic imperatives can lead to the suppression or distortion of public opinion, thereby diluting the impact of popular voices on political outcomes. The implications of this disconnect are far-reaching in democratic societies. When public opinion is stifled by industry-backed or politically motivated media discourse, the very essence of representative governance is compromised. Policies that should reflect the real needs and aspirations of the population risk being shaped by special interests, thereby undermining the fundamental principles of democracy.

Therefore, it is clear that bridging the gap between public opinion and policymaking is crucial for preserving democratic ideals and facilitating informed decision-making. To remedy this fundamental disparity, a thorough reassessment of media practices and regulatory frameworks is necessary. Promoting greater transparency, ethical journalism, and independence from special interests would enable the media to realign public discourse with policymaking, ensuring that citizens' voices play a prominent role in shaping governance. Furthermore, enhancing media literacy and promoting diversity of viewpoints can empower the public to distinguish authentic information from biased narratives, thereby reinforcing the symbiotic relationship between public opinion and policy implementation. Ultimately, rebalancing public opinion and policy requires a concerted effort to deconstruct the link between economic and geopolitical influences that permeate the media landscape, thereby affirming the primacy of democratic values in governance.

Towards transparency: reforming the links between media and politics

Examining the complex network of relationships between the media and politics reveals that the interplay of power and influence has perpetuated a system characterised by secrecy and special interests. The need for transparency in this area is not merely a matter of theoretical idealism; it is essential to preserving democratic principles and ensuring the fair representation of public interests. The complex interplay between economic incentives and editorial freedom within media institutions underscores the gravity of the issue.

Corporate ownership and advertising revenues exert considerable influence over news content and presentation, often favouring sensationalism and commercial viability at the expense of in-depth reporting. This not only distorts public discourse but also widens the gap between authentic public opinion and media representation. Furthermore, the geopolitical dimensions of media reform cannot be overlooked.

Analysing the underlying currents of foreign policy impulses and strategic alliances reveals the complexity of the media's role in promoting specific agendas. Examining the connections between economic actors, policymakers, and media conglomerates reveals a landscape where national and international interests sometimes converge at the expense of impartial and comprehensive journalism.

Reforming this landscape requires multidimensional approaches aimed at mitigating the undue influence of financial entities and strengthening media accountability. One approach to reform would be to strengthen regulatory mechanisms to protect journalistic integrity from commercial pressures while encouraging diversity of ownership models to guard against monopolisation and partisan manipulation. Additionally, fostering media literacy and encouraging critical news consumption can empower the public to discern propagandistic discourse and demand more nuanced reporting. Prioritising transparency in media ownership structures, funding sources, and conflicts of interest is essential to restore public trust in journalistic institutions and affirm their crucial role as public watchdogs and informants.

Ultimately, promoting transparency in the links between the media and politics can lead to a civic renaissance that revitalises democratic governance. By removing obstacles to honest and responsible journalism, society can foster an informed citizenry capable of guiding political discourse and shaping policies that truly reflect the public interest.

9
Occupation and Colonial Expansion
American Coverage of Israeli Wars and Colonisation Projects

A Legacy of Conflict: Tracing the Historical Roots

The Israeli-Palestinian conflict is deeply rooted in a history of territorial disputes, power struggles, and conflicting narratives. This enduring legacy can be traced back to pivotal events such as the 1917 Balfour Declaration, which promised a national home for the Jewish people in Palestine and simultaneously sparked apprehension and dissent among the indigenous Palestinian population. The subsequent waves of Jewish immigration and land acquisition laid the groundwork for mounting tensions, which culminated in the Arab-Israeli War of 1948–1949, characterised by territorial redrawing and significant population displacement.

Subsequent wars and conflicts, notably the Six-Day War in 1967 and the Yom Kippur War in 1973, further reinforced the contested status of crucial territories such as the West Bank, the Gaza Strip and East Jerusalem. Each chapter of this saga bears the mark of deeply rooted claims to historical, religious, and cultural heritage, creating a climate of conflict and endurance that shapes contemporary politics and alliances. As economic and geopolitical interests intertwine with historical grievances, the relentless struggle for dominance and survival perpetuates a cycle of occupation and resistance that resonates both locally and internationally.

The strategic value of land and power: American interests in the region

Throughout history, the Middle East has been a region of considerable geopolitical significance due to its strategic location at the intersection of Europe, Asia, and Africa. The United States' interest in the region is multifaceted and deeply rooted in economic and geopolitical considerations. The region is rich in natural resources, particularly oil, which makes it a crucial element in global energy dynamics. Control of these resources has a direct impact on the economic prosperity and national security of the United States and its allies. Additionally, the Middle East is a vital gateway for trade and commerce, further emphasising its pivotal role in international relations. Furthermore, the US government views this region as a key player in the context of broader global power struggles.

As new powers and ideological rivals rise to challenge for influence in the Middle East, maintaining a strong US presence in the region strengthens its global position. Strategic partnerships and military installations in countries such as Israel and Saudi Arabia project American power and provide leverage against adversaries.

The territory is also of paramount importance in geopolitics. Control of the territory, particularly in the context of the Israeli–Palestinian conflict, is a symbol of power and legitimacy. By supporting Israel's expansion into disputed territories, the United States not only serves its strategic interests but also reinforces its values of supporting democratic allies in the region. This alliance promotes stability and enables the United States to influence regional dynamics.

The Middle East plays a crucial role in global security architecture. The United States views its presence in the region as a counterweight to radical ideologies and terrorist threats, thereby safeguarding its territory and its allies. Policies that support the establishment of military bases, the provision of weapons and financial aid to allied nations therefore create a network of mutual security interests that strengthen the United States' geopolitical positioning.

Ultimately, US involvement in the Middle East is closely linked to deeply rooted economic and geopolitical imperatives. The region's resources, strategic partnerships, and security alliances are integral to US foreign policy, reflecting a complex interplay of power, money, and national interests.

Unwavering support: analysis of military and financial aid

The United States' unwavering support for Israel extends beyond mere diplomatic gestures, translating into substantial military and financial aid. This strategic alliance is deeply rooted in mutual geopolitical interests and economic considerations. It is therefore crucial to analyse the complex network of incentives underlying this support.

Geopolitically, Israel is a crucial ally for the United States in the unstable Middle East. However, this instability was initially caused by colonial forces (Britain and France) and the arbitrary division of Arab territories (the Sykes–Picot Agreement), followed by the establishment of an aggressive, expansionist foreign entity (Israel) at a time when Western colonisation was withdrawing from the region due to nationalist resistance.

Israel's strategic positioning enables the United States to exert its influence and counterbalance perceived threats in the region. Furthermore, safeguarding American geopolitical interests by maintaining a stable and militarily dominant Israel forms part of the broader objectives of American foreign policy. Economically, the ties between the United States and Israel are manifold.

This alliance offers substantial economic benefits. Military aid to Israel translates into lucrative defence contracts for American companies, stimulating the national economy and creating job opportunities. Additionally, technological advances and innovations resulting from military cooperation have economic value for both nations, creating a symbiotic relationship that is difficult to disentangle. Moreover, financial aid to Israel is based on strategic and economic considerations. By strengthening Israel's economy and military power, the United States can maintain its dominant position in the region and secure a lucrative market for American goods and services.

As we examine the complexities of military and financial aid more closely, it becomes evident that the alliance between the United States and Israel extends beyond mere political rhetoric. It is a calculated strategy based on shared geopolitical objectives, economic incentives and the consolidation of neo-colonial power in a region that has already experienced colonisation. These factors confirm the enduring nature of this relationship and highlight the profound impact of money and power on international policymaking.

Political symbiosis: lobbying efforts and policy formulation

The complex relationship between lobbying efforts and policy formulation lies at the intersection of economic incentives and geopolitical interests. Throughout history, interest groups and lobbyists have played a pivotal role in shaping US foreign policy, particularly in the context of the Israeli–Palestinian conflict. The political symbiosis between pro-Israel lobbying organisations, such as AIPAC, and policymakers highlights the pervasive influence of money and strategic alignment on decision-making processes. Lobbying efforts are often fuelled by substantial financial resources, which are used to influence politicians, sponsor political campaigns and organise grassroots support. This financial leverage enables lobbying groups to establish a substantial presence in Washington, thereby amplifying their voice and increasing their impact on policy decisions.

Furthermore, the reciprocity between certain lobbying entities and policymakers creates a mutual dependency whereby contributions and support from interest groups can directly influence the formulation and implementation of policies that favour specific agendas. The deep connection between economic interests and geopolitical strategies is evident in the symbiotic relationship between lobbying efforts and policy formulation. It should be noted that economic interdependence extends beyond direct financial contributions to include lucrative defence contracts and commercial collaborations that are closely linked to geopolitical imperatives.

In the case of Israel, the strategic importance of its military capabilities — obtained through the West for the aforementioned reasons — and its regional and international alliances have made it a focal point for US geopolitical interests. Consequently, the mutually beneficial partnership between American policymakers and pro-Israel lobby groups has resulted in the prioritisation and perpetuation of policies that align with Israel's security and expansionist goals.

To understand the broader implications of this political symbiosis, it is necessary to explore the multiple dimensions of power and influence, which extend beyond financial transactions to encompass diplomacy, security, and global stability. This complex interaction highlights the intricate dynamics underlying the intersection of money, interests, and politics, marking a crucial aspect of contemporary international relations.

The economics of occupation: the commercial stakes of defence contracts

In the context of US support for Israeli wars and settlement projects, the economics of occupation is a complex and multifaceted issue combining political motivations and economic interests. Fundamentally, the business of defence contracts in this area reflects the intersection of financial imperatives, power dynamics, and strategic calculations.

Geopolitically, the United States has cultivated close ties with Israel, positioning the Zionist entity as a key ally in a turbulent region. This relationship, reinforced by military aid and advanced weaponry, serves to secure American influence and pave the way for lucrative defence contracts. The deep economic collaboration between the United States and Israel extends beyond mere trade to encompass a symbiotic network of defence industry giants, political figures, and special interest groups. Profit-driven defence contractors actively influence political outcomes through lobbying and electoral contributions, perpetuating a cycle of military spending and resource allocation. The economic stakes are undeniably high, underpinning an interconnected network of relationships between the defence industry, government agencies, and pro-Israel advocacy groups.

It is worth noting that the financial implications extend far beyond national borders, resonating within the broader context of the global arms trade and economic interdependence. As the link between militarism and commerce persists, economic incentives and strategic objectives increasingly influence decision-making, affecting military aid, arms sales and international agreements. Furthermore, the convergence of economic levers and geopolitical interests fuels a discourse of mutual benefits, obscuring the real costs and consequences of sustained occupation and expansion. Therefore, it is necessary to unravel these complex economic currents and shed light on the underlying forces guiding US policy towards Israel and the Middle East in general.

Geopolitical imperatives: balancing regional allies

In the complex arena of international relations, the geopolitical imperatives that guide a nation's foreign policy are numerous and constantly evolving. When examining US-Israel relations in the context of regional alliances, it is evident that strategic interests play a pivotal role in diplomatic decisions. The geostrategic importance of the Middle East, characterised by its significant oil reserves and position at the crossroads of global trade routes, has always attracted the attention of world powers seeking to secure influence and resources. For the United States, maintaining strong ties with Israel is an essential part of its overall regional strategy. This alliance provides military advantages and intelligence cooperation, serving as a bulwark against perceived adversaries and potential disruptions to the flow of energy resources.

Furthermore, the intricate web of alliances and rivalries in the Middle East necessitates that the United States strike a delicate balance in its relations with other pivotal actors, including Saudi Arabia, Egypt, and Turkey. Each of these regional powers wields considerable influence in its own sphere, and the United States uses its alliances strategically to preserve its own influence and promote its own interests. However, achieving this balance is often challenging, particularly when competing priorities and divergent agendas arise among these allies. Furthermore, the ongoing Israeli–Palestinian conflict adds another layer of complexity. US policy must therefore strike a delicate balance between supporting Israel and negotiating peace and maintaining stability in the region — two objectives that have been mutually exclusive to date because of the nature of the Zionist project as a colonial entity that always requires more territory at the expense of the Arabs, whether in Palestine, Syria, Lebanon or wherever it perceives a vacuum.

From an economic perspective, these geopolitical imperatives are further emphasised by considerations relating to access to resources, trade partnerships and the region's overall security architecture. The interconnected nature of the global economy means that decisions regarding alliances and interventions can have a significant impact on the economic health and stability of nations. In this context, the United States' commitment to Israel is not only a matter of ideological solidarity but also a strategic neo-colonialist investment with profound economic implications, as both parties seek to strengthen their positions in an economically vital yet unstable region.

As the geopolitical landscape continues to evolve, balancing regional alliances remains a central challenge for American policymakers. Navigating the intersecting interests and dynamics of the Middle East requires astute diplomatic manoeuvring, a judicious assessment of geopolitical realities and a nuanced understanding of the economic and strategic imperatives at stake. The complexity of managing these alliances highlights the United States' pivotal role in shaping the region's trajectory, reflecting the enduring importance of geopolitical pragmatism in foreign policy.

Diplomacy at a standstill: UN resolutions and American vetoes

The United Nations, often seen as a beacon of hope for resolving diplomatic conflicts, has repeatedly encountered deadlock regarding Israel, as evidenced by resolutions criticising its actions in the Palestinian territories. During these deliberations, the US has consistently exercised its veto power in the UN Security Council to shield Israel from any censure or punitive measures, despite its war crimes. The consequences of these vetoes extend beyond mere support; they demonstrate the interplay of political influence, financial backing, and neo-colonial strategic interests.

The American diplomatic position towards Israel is based on multiple motivations. Firstly, the United States considers Israel not only as an ally but also as a vital means of preserving its influence in the Middle East. With regional stability and the protection of key economic and military assets at stake, the close relationship between the two nations takes precedence over international consensus.

Furthermore, the economic implications cannot be overlooked, with major defence contracts, technological partnerships, and market access playing a significant role in the relationship between the two countries. The United States' repeated use of the veto power raises questions and debates about the nature of its commitment to fair and impartial global governance. Impartial observers — and their numbers are growing, even within the US Congress today — argue that the continued protection of Israel through these vetoes is contrary to the principles of justice and accountability enshrined in the United Nations framework. This is causing discontent among many member states who perceive a selective application of justice, thereby undermining the institution's effectiveness and legitimacy.

Despite growing pressure, the United States continues to assert that its unwavering support for Israel aligns with its national interests and broader strategic imperatives. This view persists even in the face of evolving geopolitical changes and the increasing popularity of alternative approaches to regional peace and stability.

Thus, the status quo presents a persistent dilemma, laden

with supposedly 'diplomatic and pragmatic' considerations that resonate far beyond the halls of the UN General Assembly. The systematic use of the American veto reflects a complex web of geopolitical calculations, economic incentives, and historical allegiances. Beneath the surface of diplomatic discourse, power dynamics shaped by financial investments, military cooperation, and shared geopolitical aspirations exert a profound influence. Successfully navigating these contours requires unwavering attention to the profound interplay between money, politics, and global power dynamics, transcending conventional paradigms of international relations.

Voices of opposition: grassroots movements challenge the status quo

Voices rising against established policies in favour of Israeli occupation and expansion have emerged from grassroots movements across the United States. Composed of diverse coalitions and individuals, these movements represent a current of dissent against the status quo, posing a persistent challenge to the dominant discourse that shapes US foreign policy in the Middle East. They often highlight the humanitarian consequences of occupation and expansion, drawing attention to human rights violations and the region's destabilisation. They emphasise the moral imperative to uphold justice, equality and self-determination for all parties involved. Furthermore, they closely examine the role of political influence and financial contributions in perpetuating these policies, critically examining the interaction between economic interests, campaign financing, and decision-making in the corridors of power.

These movements' ability to catalyse change at the local level, mobilise communities, and stimulate public debate on complex geopolitical issues is what sets them apart. By leveraging social media, community events, educational initiatives and awareness campaigns, these movements amplify alternative narratives and ensure that divergent viewpoints reach a wider audience. They engage in constructive dialogue with policymakers, conducting direct outreach and urging a re-examination of US support for Israeli actions and policies in the region.

Despite formidable opposition from lobbying entities and established power structures, these grassroots movements persist in their efforts. Their resilience reflects their unwavering commitment to challenging conventional wisdom and driving positive change. As they grow in popularity, their ability to shape public opinion and influence the political landscape becomes increasingly significant. The diversity within these movements enriches the discourse, offering fresh perspectives and compelling critiques that deserve consideration. Furthermore, these movements bear witness to the democratic ideals on which the United States was founded, demonstrating the power of civic engagement and the exercise of fundamental rights. By fostering informed and passionate debate, they reinforce the principles of transparency, accountability and ethical governance in foreign policy and international relations.

In short, the voices of opposition emerging from popular movements play a vital role in holding those in power to account, promoting a more nuanced and holistic approach to the multifaceted issues surrounding Israeli occupation and expansion. Their commitment to justice, human rights and diplomatic dialogue is a transformative force that changes the way the United States engages with the Middle East.

The media: shaping perceptions of expansionism

The media plays a central role in shaping public perceptions of geopolitical events, including expansionism and occupation. In the context of US support for Israeli wars and settlement projects, the influence of the media is immense. From framing the narrative to determining which voices are amplified, media institutions have considerable power to shape public opinion.

Economic and financial interests also come into play, as media ownership and advertising revenue can impact coverage of international affairs. Conglomerates with diverse business relationships, including with defence contractors and entities invested in Israeli settlements, may be inclined to present a narrative that aligns with their broader financial interests. Geopolitical considerations also influence media narratives, as maintaining strategic alliances and partnerships is often a priority.

Regional allies of the United States, including Israel, may benefit from favourable media portrayals to help maintain diplomatic relations and military cooperation. Furthermore, the repercussions of critical reporting on Israel's actions may extend beyond the immediate context to impact other geopolitical objectives.

A complex network of influences dictates media coverage of expansionism and occupation. Highlighting the interplay between economic and geopolitical factors, as well as journalistic practices, helps us understand these dynamics. This enables us to discern the underlying forces that shape public discourse and the framing of complex geopolitical realities more clearly. Studying how the media presents expansionism reveals the mechanisms of information dissemination and the interdependence of political, economic, and media interests.

Prospects: navigating change amid growing complexity

One of the most significant challenges is navigating the complexities of US support for Israeli occupation and expansion. The deep intertwining of economic and geopolitical interests that underpin this relationship has important implications for the evolving global political landscape.

Economically, the links between defence contracts, technological innovation and strategic alliances determine the direction of US foreign policy in the Middle East. The connection between corporate influence, financial power and governmental decision-making highlights the intricacy of this geopolitical equation.

Geopolitically, new power dynamics continue to emerge on the world stage, and shifting alliances and regional dynamics further complicate prospects for change in US–Israel relations. The interplay between American interests, regional stability and broader geopolitical objectives highlights the complex interconnection of the factors influencing the way forward.

Furthermore, as public opinion and political discourse evolve, voices advocating for justice and equity are growing stronger. Grassroots movements and civil society initiatives are challenging the status quo, leading to a critical reassessment of the consequences of continued support for Israeli expansion and occupation.

Ethical considerations, human rights imperatives and moral obligations are increasingly shaping the discourse surrounding US policy in the region.

Amid these intersecting forces, the United Nations continues to play a central role in the dialogue surrounding the Israeli-Palestinian conflict as a platform for international diplomacy and multilateral engagement.

Despite persistent challenges, the need to find diplomatic solutions and uphold international law remains the cornerstone of global efforts to navigate deeply entrenched complexities.

Given these multiple dimensions, the prospects for US involvement in Israeli occupation and expansion require a holistic assessment encompassing economic, geopolitical, ethical and diplomatic considerations. The interplay of power dynamics, strategic imperatives and the defence of public interests will undoubtedly shape the way forward, presenting challenges and opportunities for positive change amid these growing complexities.

10
The Erosion of American Credibility
The Global Perception of Hypocrisy

The Changing Perception of Global Power

This shift in perception has had a profound impact on the United States' position in international affairs. Although economic and geopolitical interests still influence political decisions, the traditional power structures that once determined global influence are being reshaped by emerging powers and shifting alliances. The rise of countries such as China, India and Brazil has challenged the historically dominant role of Western nations, resulting in a more multipolar world order. This shift poses new challenges for the United States as it seeks to maintain its position as a global leader. The interaction between economic globalisation and strategic interests significantly influences how nations perceive American power and policies. The interconnectedness of the global economy has increased the importance of economic leverage in international relations.

In this context, financial flows and investments have become essential tools for exerting influence and shaping diplomatic outcomes. Furthermore, the close relationship between economic prosperity and national security has led the United States to prioritise economic interests in its foreign policy decisions. Geopolitical considerations also play a crucial role in the perception of global power.

The strategic importance of regions such as the Middle East and Asia has led to intense competition among major powers, each seeking to exert influence and control. This struggle for geopolitical dominance has implications for how the world perceives the United States' role in these regions.

As economic and military resources are deployed to advance strategic objectives, the international community scrutinises the United States' actions and motivations closely. These shifts in global power dynamics underscore the importance of understanding the complex interplay among economic, geopolitical, and diplomatic factors that influence international perceptions of the United States. Therefore, a nuanced understanding of these multifaceted dynamics is crucial to comprehending the evolving landscape of global power politics and its implications for U.S. foreign policy.

Underlying financial currents: funding and influence

In politics and international relations, financial influence is a powerful force. Economic powers and corporations exert considerable influence over government decisions, shaping policies that align with their economic and geopolitical interests. The relationships between lobbyists, corporations and political figures create a complex web of influence where financial contributions often dictate policy direction.

This reality underscores the profound impact of money on political decisions, highlighting how it can undermine the integrity of diplomatic relations and the pursuit of global stability. Understanding the deep interaction between underlying financial currents and political decision-making is crucial to grasping the erosion of American credibility in the eyes of the international community.

As financial resources flow into political campaigns and initiatives, special interests often take precedence over broader diplomatic and ethical governance goals. Furthermore, the strategic allocation of funds to specific foreign policies serves to advance economic agendas and consolidate geopolitical positions, often at the expense of ethical considerations or the long-term repercussions on international relations. This intricate interplay between funding and influence transcends domestic affairs, permeating the foreign policy landscape and shaping alliances and allegiances on the global stage. This reflects the interdependent nature of economic power and political manoeuvring, where financial incentives have considerable power to redirect the course of international relations and reshape perceptions of credibility and trust. Shedding light on these underlying financial currents and the conflicts of interest they engender is essential to understanding the complexities of American foreign policy and the motivations behind diplomatic positions and manoeuvres.

From ally to critic: the changing international outlook

The changing international outlook towards the United States is a subject of growing attention and debate. Once regarded as the champions of democracy and freedom, the United States has undergone a notable shift in perception on the world stage. This transformation is heavily influenced by economic and geopolitical interests, as well as the role of money in shaping policy and alliances.

The complex interaction between economic interests and diplomatic strategies is evident in the evolution of international relations. Underlying financial currents, which are often hidden from the general public, play a central role in the decisions and actions of the United States and its allies. Furthermore, as economic and geopolitical issues intensify, the complexity of international alliances and interests increases, too.

As the world witnesses these changes, former allies have begun to criticise US policies and behaviour, partly motivated by their own economic and strategic interests. Delicately balanced relationships are shifting as countries weigh their economic dependencies against their ideological affinities. Power dynamics are continually shaped by financial interests, which often take precedence over traditional diplomatic strategies.

This shift impacts not only bilateral relations but also has broader implications for global stability. It is crucial to recognise the significant impact of money and economic interests on the redefinition of alliances and the reshaping of international perceptions. The emerging landscape requires a nuanced understanding of the inherent tensions between economic priorities and diplomatic principles. As nations recalibrate their positions in this new paradigm, the traditional concepts of allies and adversaries are undergoing profound transformation. The international community's perception of the United States is inextricably linked to the complex interplay between economic and geopolitical interests. Understanding these changes is essential for navigating the ever-evolving landscape of global politics and diplomacy.

Economic interests versus diplomatic strategy

The interaction between the two is the cornerstone of international relations and often shapes nations' foreign policy. In the context of the United States, this dynamic balance has been the subject of intense scrutiny and debate. Aligning economic agendas with diplomatic initiatives is a complex puzzle where profit and power intersect.

At its core, this convergence embodies a powerful blend of national and commercial interests, blurring the lines between governance and financial gain. The allure of economic gain can significantly influence a nation's diplomatic inclinations. Corporations, which have considerable economic power, seek to influence foreign policy decisions in ways that align with their profit motives.

The considerable impact of lobbying efforts and financial contributions on policymakers and their strategic manoeuvring on the global stage cannot be overstated. This symbiotic relationship between economic powers and political actors raises pertinent questions about the true drivers of diplomatic actions and decisions.

Furthermore, the pursuit of economic interests can conflict with broader diplomatic strategies, as prioritising short-term gains can clash with long-term geopolitical objectives. The allure of trade agreements, market access and lucrative investment opportunities can sometimes overshadow considerations of collective security, human rights and sustainable development. In such cases, economic imperatives can compromise diplomatic integrity, undermining a nation's moral authority and credibility on the world stage.

Conversely, diplomatic strategies also strongly influence economic dynamics, with alliances, sanctions, and regional stability initiatives directly impacting trade relations and the investment climate. The balance between asserting influence through a military presence and promoting economic partnerships highlights the complex relationship between national interests and global interdependence.

Geopolitical calculations further complicate this landscape as competing powers vie for dominance, leveraging their resources to advance their respective economic and security agendas. The intersection of economic interests and diplomatic strategy requires critical examination to shed light on the subtle undercurrents that drive international relations. To truly understand the motivations behind political decisions, it is necessary to trace the complex web of economic relationships and geopolitical manoeuvring that shapes global governance.

Media representation and public opinion abroad

Media representation and public opinion abroad play a central role in the global perception of American credibility. In today's interconnected media landscape, information and narratives spread rapidly across borders, influencing public opinion and government policy.

The influence of economic and geopolitical interests on media representation is significant. Financial considerations often incentivise the media to align with or promote narratives that serve the interests of powerful entities. Furthermore, economic ties and strategic alliances can result in biased reporting or selective coverage, providing international audiences with an incomplete or distorted picture.

This manipulation of information can have far-reaching repercussions. It affects how people around the world perceive the actions and decisions of the US government. Additionally, the impact of political lobbying and corporate influence on media messaging must not be overlooked. Powerful interest groups use their financial resources to influence the presentation of international affairs, often favouring their own agendas over objective reporting.

This dynamic impacts not only the representation of US foreign policy, but also how global events and conflicts are presented. Consequently, public opinion abroad is shaped by a complex interplay of economic, political and strategic interests, creating an environment in which genuine understanding and impartial analysis can be overshadowed by special interests. The ramifications of this biased representation extend beyond mere perception; they can directly impact diplomatic relations, trade agreements and international cooperation. It is crucial to recognise the various factors that influence media representation and public opinion abroad, as these factors significantly impact how the United States is perceived and engaged with on the world stage.

Military alliances and their unintended consequences

Military alliances play a significant role in global geopolitics and international relations. These partnerships often stem from mutual defence agreements, economic interests, and shared ideological positions. However, the repercussions of these alliances can be far-reaching, affecting not only the parties involved but also the geopolitical landscape as a whole.

At the heart of these alliances lie money and power, with nations leveraging their economic and military capabilities to cement strategic partnerships. Historically, powerful nations have strengthened their geopolitical influence and advanced their economic agendas by supporting allied states. This influence often extends to policymaking and decision-making processes within allied countries, marking a departure from truly autonomous governance.

The deep-rooted economic foundations of military alliances can significantly influence foreign policy decisions, leading to actions that prioritise financial benefits over moral or ethical considerations. Furthermore, the interdependence of economic interests and military cooperation can perpetuate a cycle of dependency in which smaller nations become indebted to larger powers within the alliance.

The repercussions of military alliances are manifold and extend beyond mere economic entanglements. Geopolitically, these agreements can contribute to regional instability and the escalation of conflicts. By extending their military presence and influence through alliance networks, powerful nations may inadvertently fuel tensions and rivalries with other global powers. Furthermore, the complexity of military alliances can exacerbate existing regional conflicts, potentially intensifying proxy wars and hindering diplomatic efforts to resolve disputes. The conflicting interests and objectives of different alliance members create additional layers of complexity, often resulting in divergent policies and strategies that strain diplomatic relations and hinder a unified global approach to conflict resolution.

Thus, the unintended consequences of military alliances highlight the complex interplay between economic incentives, geopolitical manoeuvring and the evolving nature of global power dynamics. Policymakers and analysts must recognise these complexities to understand the implications of military collaboration and its profound impact on regional stability and international relations.

Geopolitical Calculations and Regional Stability

Within the complex web of global politics, geopolitical calculations play a central role in regional stability. The interplay between economic interests, military alliances and diplomatic strategies often determines the direction of a nation's policies. Money influences the course of international relations as countries seek to protect their economic investments and advance their long-term strategic objectives.

In their quest for regional dominance and control of resources, many countries engage in calculated manoeuvres that have profound implications for stability. Economic powers compete to exert influence in strategically vital regions, leveraging their financial clout to gain geopolitical advantage. This relentless pursuit of supremacy frequently causes political friction and exacerbates existing conflicts, contributing to regional instability.

Furthermore, the intersection of economic and geopolitical interests often means that strategic alliances are prioritised over human rights concerns. Nations may turn a blind eye to human rights violations or undemocratic practices to maintain partnerships that serve their economic and security interests. Such compromises highlight the enduring importance of economic and strategic considerations in foreign policymaking, often at the expense of ethics.

The complex balance of power in unstable regions relies on the intricate interplay between economic and security motivations. Geopolitical calculations determine policies aimed at maintaining regional stability, which sometimes necessitate difficult compromises and conditional commitments. These calculations illustrate the harsh reality of international relations, where the pursuit of economic and geopolitical interests frequently takes precedence over broader humanitarian and ethical considerations.

As the global landscape continues to evolve, it is crucial to grasp the intricate dynamics of these calculations and their repercussions on regional stability. Delving deeper into the motivations behind political decisions provides valuable insight into the forces that shape international relations, helping us to better understand the complexity of the geopolitical landscape.

Human rights relegated to the background: political priorities

The prioritisation of economic and geopolitical interests has often led to human rights being overlooked in US foreign policy. This reflects a broader trend in which pragmatic considerations, such as trade agreements, military alliances, and strategic partnerships, take precedence over humanitarian concerns in decision-making processes.

The influence of money and economic interests in setting these priorities cannot be underestimated. Economic ties with certain countries or regions can lead policymakers to overlook human rights violations to maintain favourable diplomatic and economic relations.

Geopolitical considerations also play an important role in relegating human rights to the background of political agendas. The pursuit of regional stability and security frequently leads the United States to support regimes that are known to violate human rights, particularly when those regimes align with US strategic interests.

This realist approach can result in ethical and human rights considerations being overlooked in favour of maintaining a balance of power and influence in key regions of the globe. Furthermore, the nature of international power dynamics complicates the implementation of human rights as a top priority.

As emerging global powers assert their economic and political influence, the United States often faces challenges in promoting human rights without compromising its strategic positioning or economic partnerships. This dynamic highlights the complex interaction between economic incentives, geopolitical calculations and the promotion of human rights on the international stage.

Moreover, media coverage of human rights issues abroad often reflects political priorities, thereby shaping public opinion and influencing government action. When certain human rights violations receive limited media coverage, they may not capture the attention of the public or policymakers, allowing economic and geopolitical interests to take precedence.

This alignment of media discourse with political priorities contributes to the continued marginalisation of human rights issues in foreign policy decision-making. Essentially, the relegation of human rights in American politics can be attributed to a complex network of economic, geopolitical, and media influences. The challenge lies in reconciling these competing pressures with the moral imperative to uphold universal human rights standards, particularly in a world where economic and strategic interests profoundly impact international relations.

Reactions from emerging world powers

The emergence of new world powers, such as China and India, poses a significant challenge to the traditional dominance of American leadership. These rising powers have begun to assert themselves in world affairs, not only economically, but also politically and militarily. Their responses to American policies, particularly those perceived as being driven by economic and geopolitical interests, have played a decisive role in shaping the contemporary international landscape.

One notable response has been the strategic alliances formed by these emerging powers to counter American influence. Through significant economic investment and diplomatic manoeuvring, they have sought to expand their spheres of influence, thereby challenging the long-standing hegemony of the United States. At the heart of these reactions lies a complex web of economic and geopolitical calculations. Shifting global trade and investment dynamics have given rise to competition and cooperation between established and emerging powers. Economic incentives and strategic alliances are used as tools to shape policies that serve these nations' interests.

Furthermore, the quest for control over vital resources and markets, which often intersects with the geopolitical ambitions of these emerging powers, has fuelled their responses to US policy decisions even further. The rhetoric and actions of these powers can be interpreted as a calculated response to perceived US hypocrisy and self-interest.

These nations have not overlooked cases of double standards and selective enforcement of human rights and democratic principles, leading them to emphasise the importance of sovereignty and non-interference in internal affairs. This defensive stance highlights their determination to counter any attempts to impose values and norms that solely serve American interests.

The response of emerging global powers forms part of a broader discourse of ideological competition and divergent visions of the world order. As they gain prominence on the global stage, their efforts to challenge and recalibrate American leadership reflect differences in approach and conflicting aspirations for the future of the international system. This landscape of competing power dynamics and shifting allegiances is a testament to the enduring influence and complexity of global politics, where economic and geopolitical interests intersect to shape the responses and strategies of emerging world powers.

11
The Dream of a Greater Israel and the Role of the United States
Netanyahu's Vision and Washington's Policy

Introduction to the Vision of Greater Israel

The concept of Greater Israel stems from deeply rooted ideological and theological beliefs that significantly impact the political landscape of the Middle East. At its core, the vision of Greater Israel stems from a narrative with significant religious and historical importance, shaping the perspectives of Israeli policymakers and influencing their approach to territorial expansion and settlement activities.

From a political science perspective, grasping the historical context of this vision is crucial for understanding decision-making and policymaking processes within Israel, as well as its interactions with other regional nations. The notion of Greater Israel encompasses the pursuit of territorial expansion and the promotion of exclusive Jewish sovereignty over these territories. This is intrinsically linked to geopolitical interests and has profound implications for regional stability, international relations and the ongoing Israeli–Palestinian conflict. Furthermore, examining the economic incentives underlying the pursuit of Greater Israel reveals the intricate relationship between financial interests, control of resources and the perpetuation of occupation as a means of consolidating power and influence.

The discourse surrounding the Greater Israel vision is framed by the intertwining of theological imperatives, historical narratives, and strategic objectives, highlighting the multiple dimensions of this complex geopolitical phenomenon. We will therefore pause here to conduct an in-depth analysis of the foundations of the Greater Israel concept, elucidating the convergence of ideological, theological and pragmatic factors that have brought this vision to the forefront of Israeli politics and foreign policy considerations.

Historical context: Understanding Netanyahu's political ideology

Benjamin Netanyahu's extremist political ideology has been shaped by a historical context encompassing personal experiences and deeply held perspectives on Israel's role in the Middle East.

Resilience and autonomy have become core values in his worldview, strongly influencing his approach to governance and foreign policy. His early exposure to the repercussions of the Arab-Israeli conflict, particularly the Six-Day War of 1967 and its aftermath, instilled in him a sense of urgency regarding the acquisition of territory through force and military power. This formative period also coincided with Israel's emergence as a key player in the Cold War, further reinforcing his belief in the necessity of an assertive Zionist stance.

His time in the elite Sayeret Matkal unit of the Israeli Defence Forces added a pragmatic and strategic dimension to his perspective, emphasising the importance of military deterrence and proactive defence. Furthermore, Netanyahu's academic studies and subsequent professional career enabled him to refine his political acumen and deepen his understanding of international relations. His time at MIT and subsequent work in consulting and diplomacy reinforced his understanding of economic interdependence and geopolitical power dynamics.

His political, economic and ideological vision, informed by the Israeli far right from Ze'ev Jabotinsky to Menachem Begin, is inseparable from his geopolitical ambitions, particularly about the occupation and expansion of Israeli settlements in the West Bank. The quest for strategic territorial control has become intertwined with economic imperatives, revealing a multifaceted agenda that blurs the lines between security, economic prosperity, and ideological fervour. Those who analyse its actions and policies must untangle the complex interplay of historical and ideological legacies, strategic imperatives, and economic factors to understand its extreme decisions, which show no regard for international law or human rights — let alone the women and children it bombs.

Economic incentives: the business of occupation and expansion

The economic incentives that motivate the occupation and expansion of territories in the context of Israel's vision of greater regional influence cannot be underestimated. The financial ramifications of maintaining control over disputed lands, such as the West Bank and the Golan Heights, have significant implications for Israeli and international stakeholders alike.

From an economic standpoint, settlements in these regions are lucrative for Israeli businesses and investors, frequently at the expense of Palestinian livelihoods. Furthermore, a complex network of economic interests is closely tied to the political landscape, blurring the lines between state policy and private gain. The Israeli government's financial incentives to promote settlement construction and expansion have created a lucrative market for industries that benefit from territorial control, including real estate, agriculture, and infrastructure development. This economic programme fuels the perpetuation of the occupation and reinforces the power and prosperity of the Israeli state and its allies. It is important to emphasise 'its allies' because they are complicit in Israel's crimes.

Furthermore, the geopolitical significance of these expansionist efforts cannot be overlooked. By strategically establishing settlements in disputed territories, Israel asserts its dominance and secures vital resources and strategic positions in an unstable region. The dual nature of these economic and geopolitical interests underpins the complexity of Israeli policies regarding territorial expansion and the consolidation of its presence in disputed areas.

The flow of financial aid from external sources, particularly the United States, supports the implementation of these colonial expansionist policies. Military aid and diplomatic support perpetuate Israel's control over occupied territories, demonstrating the intertwining of economic incentives and foreign policy objectives. Understanding the relationship between economic motivations and biblically inspired geopolitical ambitions sheds light on the underlying forces shaping the pursuit of Greater Israel and the contours of regional power dynamics and international alignments.

The economic drivers of occupation and expansion highlight the complex interplay of financial interests and political agendas, and encapsulate the profound repercussions for global governance and security frameworks. A thorough examination of these economic incentives reveals the multifaceted nature of Israel's strategic considerations and the enduring impact of this paradigm on regional stability and the failure of peace negotiations.

Geopolitical interests: maintaining regional dominance

In Israel's case, the quest to maintain regional dominance is deeply linked to historical conflicts and complex power dynamics. From a political science perspective, grasping the importance of maintaining regional dominance necessitates a comprehensive analysis of economic, military, and diplomatic factors. Discussions on this topic often lead to an exploration of the power struggles, alliances and complex web of influences that shape international relations in the Middle East.

To further this concept, it is essential to examine the multiple facets of geopolitical interests and their implications for the stakeholders involved. Economic incentives play a central role in shaping these interests as they often determine the extent of a nation's influence in a region. The control and exploitation of resources, trade routes and markets are essential elements in maintaining regional dominance.

In the context of Israeli policy, economic considerations overlap with territorial expansion and occupation, creating a complex landscape in which financial gains are closely linked to geopolitical objectives. Israel's strategic positioning in the Middle East further amplifies the importance of economic interests as it seeks to establish itself as a regional power.

Military supremacy and security concerns also play a significant role in maintaining regional dominance. Israel's emphasis on its military capabilities and defence strategies reflects its desire to assert its influence and deter potential adversaries.

The interplay between military might and diplomatic manoeuvring underscores the intricacies of geopolitical interests as nations navigate a turbulent landscape shaped by historical animosities and contemporary rivalries. Diplomatic initiatives and alliances are also integral to maintaining regional dominance. Leveraging political relationships and international partnerships is an essential tool for advancing geopolitical agendas. For Israel, forging alliances and securing the support of influential global players is key to consolidating its position in the Middle East.

The complexity of diplomatic manoeuvring reveals the interdependent nature of geopolitical interests, with nations constantly struggling for dominance and relevance. In short, the quest to maintain regional dominance encompasses a wide range of factors, from economic incentives to military strategies and diplomatic engagements. Understanding how these elements interact is essential to grasping the complex motivations that drive countries such as Israel to seek regional influence. Ultimately, preserving regional dominance represents the complex network of power relations and strategic calculations that characterise the Middle Eastern geopolitical landscape, particularly about a pariah state built from scratch in an imperialist factory and implanted in the heart of the Arab-Muslim world to thwart any attempt at emancipation, sovereignty, and progress for local populations.

The role of American lobbying and political campaign financing

This complex network plays a central role in the development of American foreign policy, particularly in its support for Israel and the wider Middle East region. The influence of special interest groups, including pro-Israel lobbies, on decision-making processes within the American government is immense.

Although the US claims to be a democracy, its oligarchic politics are heavily influenced by the financial resources provided by various interest groups, both domestic and international. AIPAC (the American Israel Public Affairs Committee), often considered one of the most influential lobby groups, wields considerable power thanks to its substantial financial resources and how they are used.

The economic incentives and donations provided by these interest groups to political campaigns (essentially legal bribes) reinforce the alignment of Washington's policies with Israeli objectives. By making strategic contributions to political candidates who support pro-Israel policies, these lobby groups ensure their views are represented within the legislative and executive branches of the US government. With their significant financial influence, these groups support not only candidates who favour them but also exert pressure to advance their agendas, such as providing military aid to Israel or securing diplomatic support on international platforms.

The interconnection between commercial interests and geopolitical strategies further complicates this dynamic.

Military-industrial complexes, which are closely linked to foreign policy, perpetuate the cycle of financial dependence on support for certain geopolitical aspirations. This symbiotic relationship between economic motivations and strategic alliances adds another dimension to US-Israel relations, highlighting the extent to which money and power influence decision-making processes at the highest levels of governance.

The implications of lobbying and campaign financing extend beyond the national sphere, affecting the global perception of US policies and integrity. As financial support influences political positions and policymaking, it has repercussions in international affairs, raising questions about the impartiality and autonomy of US foreign policy decisions. Furthermore, lobbying's significant influence in Washington politics has profound ramifications for the prospects of fair conflict resolution, particularly in the context of the Israeli-Palestinian conflict. Analysing the role of American lobbying and political campaign financing reveals that economic and geopolitical interests intertwine to shape policy-making. The convergence of lobbying power, financial resources and broader strategic objectives creates a complex web of influence that continues to impact the United States' commitment to Israel, despite its human rights violations. In short, the United States sponsors and protects a pariah state whose prime minister has been convicted by the International Criminal Court.

Politics in Washington: Alignment with Israeli Political Objectives

Washington's politics often reflect a complex interplay of interests, in which alignment with Israeli political objectives remains a constant and influential factor. This encompasses a multitude of considerations, ranging from historical alliances and shared security concerns to economic partnerships and ideological affinities. At the heart of this relationship lies a web of influences propagated through lobbying, election campaign financing and strategic decision-making.

The power of money in Washington should not be underestimated. Lobby groups defending Israeli political objectives have mobilised substantial financial resources to influence political discourse, shape legislation, and sway policymakers. The economic incentives behind these lobbying efforts extend beyond traditional diplomatic and strategic considerations to include commercial opportunities, arms contracts and investment initiatives, which further strengthen the ties between the United States and Israel.

It is within this network of economic interests that the true depth of Washington's alignment with Israeli objectives becomes apparent, transcending the confines of conventional geopolitical discourse. Furthermore, aligning with Israeli political objectives offers strategic advantages that align with broader US geopolitical interests. A strong alliance with Israel is essential for American influence and presence in the turbulent Middle Eastern landscape.

By providing political and military support to Israel, the United States aims to consolidate its presence in the region, influence regional dynamics, and counterbalance emerging threats. These geopolitical imperatives highlight the complexity of Washington's support for Israeli policies, which extends well beyond mere ideological solidarity. Given the multifaceted nature of this alignment, it is evident that Washington's policy is not solely guided by normative principles, but is also deeply intertwined with considerations that transcend traditional paradigms of international relations, as well as the fundamental values of the American state. The interdependent nature of economic, strategic, and ideological convergence highlights the depth of this alignment, steering US foreign policy towards ambitions that belong to a bygone era when Europe encouraged adventurers, many of whom were outlaws, to settle in America, resulting in numerous genocides against the local populations.

Media influence: crafting narratives and shaping public opinion

The media plays a central role in influencing public opinion and constructing narratives surrounding geopolitical conflicts. When it comes to the Israeli–Palestinian conflict, the power of the media cannot be underestimated. The way events are presented, questions are framed, and topics are selected can profoundly impact public perception and political decisions.

However, behind this influence lies a complex web of economic and geopolitical interests that often dictate the promoted narratives and how they are presented. A key aspect of media influence is the financial backing and ownership of major news organisations. In the case of the Israeli-Palestinian conflict, media organisations may be influenced by financial incentives related to ownership or advertising revenue. Pro-Israeli lobby groups and wealthy individuals with interests in the region may pressure media companies to present narratives that align with Israeli political objectives. This can result in biased reporting, selective coverage or the omission of critical perspectives that challenge the status quo. Additionally, economic considerations come into play through commercial partnerships and investment opportunities.

Media conglomerates with commercial interests in Israel or ties to pro-Israeli entities may engage in self-censorship or soften critical coverage to avoid jeopardising their economic relationships. The intertwining of media ownership, financial incentives, and geopolitical interests creates an environment in which certain narratives are privileged, while others are marginalised. Geopolitical considerations further amplify the impact of media discourse. For example, the United States' strategic alliance with Israel, motivated by geopolitical calculations in the Middle East, shapes how the conflict is portrayed in the American media.

Portraying Israel as a steadfast ally and bastion of democracy serves broader geopolitical interests, thereby bolstering support for US foreign policy in the region. Consequently, the media may be inclined to reinforce these narratives to align with the US government's positions and alliances. This influence extends beyond traditional news media to encompass social media, advocacy campaigns, and think tanks.

The dissemination of selected content via digital platforms and targeted messaging amplifies the reach of certain narratives, thereby helping to shape public opinion. Campaigns that leverage online influence, sponsored content and strategic messaging further blur the lines between objective information and special interests. The repercussions of media influence on the Israeli-Palestinian conflict are profound, impacting public perception, political discourse, and policymaking. Therefore, it is essential to understand the complex dynamics of media narratives and the forces that drive them in order to grasp the deeper levels of influence at play in shaping public opinion and political outcomes.

Implications for aspirations for a Palestinian state

The implications of the Greater Israel vision and its alignment with Washington's policy extend far beyond domestic politics and media influence. One of the most significant consequences is its impact on aspirations for a Palestinian state.

Unwavering support for Israeli expansion and occupation undermines the prospects for a viable Palestinian state and perpetuates the cycle of conflict and instability in the region.

Economically, the continued expansion of Israeli settlements in the West Bank and East Jerusalem poses a significant obstacle to establishing an independent Palestinian state. This deliberate encroachment limits the land available for future Palestinian sovereignty and disrupts the economic development of Palestinian communities. Control over strategic resources and key infrastructure further strengthens Israel's position, exacerbating economic inequalities between the two populations.

From a geopolitical perspective, the lack of progress towards a just and lasting resolution prolongs current tensions in the Middle East and diminishes the credibility of international efforts to negotiate peace. Failing to address the legitimate aspirations of the Palestinian people amplifies grievances and fuels radicalisation, threatening regional stability and global security.

Furthermore, the perpetuation of the Israeli-Palestinian conflict hinders the ability to cooperate on other pressing geopolitical issues, such as combating extremism and promoting human rights in the region. In the context of political influence and lobbying, systemic support for Israeli policies in Washington directly impacts diplomatic efforts to resolve the conflict. Significant financial contributions and lobbying activities by pro-Israel interest groups influence discourse and decision-making, often to the detriment of meaningful engagement with Palestinian leaders. This imbalance of influence distorts perceptions of the conflict and prevents the formulation of a balanced and fair approach to achieving a comprehensive and lasting peace agreement.

Given these multiple ramifications, the consequences for the establishment of a Palestinian state are profound. The intersection of economic interests, geopolitical calculations and political lobbying serves to reinforce and entrench the status quo, thereby undermining the prospects for a negotiated settlement that recognises the legitimate rights and aspirations of the Palestinian people.

Global reactions and international ramifications

The vision of Greater Israel and its pursuit have significant repercussions on the world stage, eliciting a wide range of reactions and causing international ramifications. The situation presents a complex web of diplomatic challenges, with countries and international organisations striving to adjust their responses while taking into account historical alliances, strategic interests, and moral imperatives.

As the primary international institution responsible for maintaining peace and security, the United Nations has been a central arena for discussions on the Israeli-Palestinian conflict. However, political and economic interests often dictate the positions of member states, making it difficult to find a solution. The disproportionate influence exerted by certain powers with veto rights over the drafting of UN resolutions highlights the impact of geopolitical agendas on seemingly impartial decision-making processes.

At the regional level, neighbouring states and long-standing allies are in a delicate position. While some countries strongly advocate the establishment of a Palestinian state and condemn Israeli expansionism, others pragmatically align themselves with Israel due to shared security concerns and mutual economic interests.

Europe faces its own internal dynamics as it seeks to balance historical guilt with contemporary political strategies. The European Union embodies this discord, as member states must reconcile their differing views while the public increasingly expects them to adopt principled stances on foreign policy matters. The recent recognition of a Palestinian state by France, Britain and other European countries is a historic event that renews hope for a negotiable solution. At the same time, however, this puts the United States in a difficult position and increasingly isolates Israel, which is criticised for its actions in Gaza.

Public opinion and civil society initiatives around the world continue to shape the discourse. Grassroots movements, advocacy groups and influential figures are using their influence to mobilise support for marginalised voices and campaign for justice. These efforts counterbalance state-centred narratives by injecting moral imperatives into political calculations and holding decision-makers to account.

As the dispute over US–Israel relations plays out in this international context, it is evident that both are under intense scrutiny for their actions. The long-standing partnership between Washington and Tel Aviv is under increased scrutiny, with critics highlighting perceived injustices and calling for a rebalancing of power. This sustained attention creates dilemmas for policymakers, forcing them to consider the long-term consequences of unquestioning support and the potential erosion of diplomatic credibility on the world stage.

Conclusion: Assessing the Long-Term Implications for US–Israel Relations

The long-term implications of US–Israel relations have been the subject of much debate and analysis in political and academic circles. It is crucial to evaluate these implications using an analytical approach that considers both historical context and contemporary dynamics.

The pervasive influence of money and special interests must be considered when evaluating the trajectory of this significant international alliance. Economic and geopolitical considerations continue to shape US–Israel relations profoundly. Economic incentives related to military aid, trade partnerships and defence contracts have fostered a close bond between the two nations.

Furthermore, Israel's strategic importance as a tool for the United States means the latter is compelled to provide ongoing support to maintain stability and influence in the region. This convergence of economic and geopolitical interests creates a complex network of interdependence in which political decisions are influenced by multiple factors.

The influence of lobbying and campaign financing on American politics is significant. AIPAC and other pro-Israel groups have considerable financial resources at their disposal, enabling them to influence the discourse in Washington and advance policies that align with Israeli objectives. Combined with effective lobbying efforts, financial flows have created an environment in which it is increasingly difficult to deviate from this established line. Consequently, the influence of money has become integral to the formulation and execution of American foreign policy, particularly regarding Israel.

To assess the long-term implications, it is necessary to thoroughly understand how these dynamics influence not only US–Israel relations, but also broader regional and global dynamics. The ramifications extend beyond bilateral relations, impacting issues such as Palestinian statehood aspirations, regional security dynamics and American credibility on the world stage. The perceived alignment with Israeli policies has elicited varied reactions from the international community, shaping global perceptions of US involvement in the Middle East and beyond.

In conclusion, as the political landscape continues to evolve, the interplay of economic, geopolitical, and lobbying influences on US-Israel relations will remain at the centre of analysis and debate. The profound implications of this alliance require ongoing examination and reflection, particularly in the context of broader international developments and the quest for a just and lasting peace in the Middle East.

12
The America that Fought Fascism No Longer Exists

Anti-Popular Wars in the Service of Big Business

Decoding the anti-fascist legacy of the United States: the idealism of past wars

Historically, the United States' involvement in fighting fascist regimes has been celebrated as evidence of its dedication to democratic principles. Echoes of the Second World War and the fight against Nazi Germany continue to resonate in contemporary political discourse, shaping perceptions of the nation's moral obligation to maintain international order and defend against totalitarian threats. This idealism has been the cornerstone of many domestic and international policy decisions, guiding the trajectory of American diplomacy and military engagements for decades.

However, the narrative of anti-fascist fervour conceals the complex interactions between economic forces and geopolitical interests. Although the rhetoric of liberation and justice permeated public discourse, lucrative economic opportunities and strategic advantages often underpinned decision-making processes behind the scenes. A closer examination reveals the intertwining of corporate and military interests, where war profits were essential to sustaining the apparatus of conflict, not merely incidental. The lure of wartime prosperity and the influence wielded by defence contractors had a considerable impact on policymaking, starkly illustrating the power of money in shaping foreign and domestic agendas.

Furthermore, the anti-fascist legacy of the United States was intimately linked to the geopolitical landscape. The identification of allies and adversaries on the world stage was not solely based on ideological alignment, but was also motivated by calculated strategic positioning. Allies were courted not only for their commitment to democratic values, but also for the strategic advantages they offered on the broader geopolitical chessboard. This pragmatic fusion of moral imperatives and strategic interests highlights the multifaceted nature of American foreign policy, reminding us that the pursuit of noble ideals often coincides with the pursuit of national interests.

As we navigate the complexities of historical idealism and realpolitik, we must ask what has become of the legacy of America's struggle against fascism. This legacy should have profound implications for contemporary political dynamics — if any continuity exists, that is. Unfortunately, however, the history of the United States since World War II does not provide a positive answer. There have been countless American wars whose goal was nothing less than superpower hegemony, achieved by any means necessary. In reality, all the wars waged by the United States since the Second World War have been imperialist wars, whose undeclared goal is to dominate countries and regions and subject them to American rule. This became particularly scandalous when Donald Trump stated that 'Israel is very small and should be enlarged'.

To analyse the lasting impact of wars on current political paradigms, it is imperative to understand the complex network of economic incentives, geopolitical manoeuvres and ideological fervour (fighting communism, overthrowing dictatorial regimes in Iraq or Libya, exporting democracy, etc.).

Economic forces and military enterprises: the profits of war

The interaction between war, economic interests, and politics has long been the subject of intense study and debate. In the context of American military history, the undeniable influence of economic forces on decision-making cannot be ignored.

Analysing the nuances of this complex relationship is essential to understanding the underlying motivations behind political choices. Despite its devastating human cost, war has often been accompanied by significant financial opportunities for certain sectors of society. Defence contractors, for instance, have substantially profited from supplying the military-industrial complex with weapons, technology and logistical support. The symbiotic relationship between the defence industry and government institutions creates a direct interest in perpetuating armed conflict. Moreover, the economic benefits of war extend beyond defence contractors to a wider network of companies linked to the war machine. Various sectors stand to gain from sustained military operations, from infrastructure construction and development to resource extraction and logistics.

Geopolitical interests further incentivise the continuation of war, with strategic positioning and control of resources guiding foreign policy decisions. Pursuing global dominance and influence often requires military intervention, which serves the economic and geopolitical objectives of key stakeholders. Consequently, political choices are closely linked to economic imperatives, with significant consequences for the course of international relations. Moreover, the discourse surrounding war and its implications is meticulously crafted to garner public support and justify military endeavours.

Media representation and discourse play a central role in shaping public perception of war, often emphasising national security interests while downplaying the economic dimensions of conflict. Thus, visible and invisible forces converge to form a complex network of motivations that blurs the lines between moral imperatives and economic incentives.

Examining this complex web of influences critically is essential to understanding the holistic nature of political decision-making. By dissecting the rhetoric and examining the fundamental factors underlying military operations, we can shed light on the underlying currents that shape our collective geopolitical landscape.

American businesses in times of war: from defence contracts to influence

During wartime, the relationship between American businesses and the government becomes increasingly close, creating a complex network of influence and power. Defence contracts form the cornerstone of these relationships, offering lucrative opportunities for companies while serving the nation's strategic interests. The interaction between economic and geopolitical factors is crucial to understanding the dynamics at work in times of war.

Recognising that defence contractors exert considerable influence over policy and decision-making through their financial contributions and lobbying efforts is crucial. Often possessing resources and capabilities coveted by the military-industrial complex, these companies can leverage their position to influence the direction of national security policy. This relationship is symbiotic: the government depends on these companies to provide the tools of war, while the companies benefit from sustained demand for their products and services. This convergence of interests raises questions about potential conflicts of interest and highlights the profound implications of prioritising profit in the realm of national security. Furthermore, the awarding of defence contracts can impact the economic landscape, with certain regions and industries reaping considerable benefits. This can influence the national political climate, as elected officials seek to respond to the interests of their constituents and preserve employment opportunities.

Geopolitical interests also come into play, as these defence contracts can cement strategic alliances and partnerships with other nations. However, the pursuit of geopolitical advantages must be carefully considered, as it can lead to entanglements that prioritise short-term gains at the expense of long-term stability and morality. As we navigate the complex web of corporate influence in times of war, it is crucial that we critically evaluate the existing power structures and examine the broader ethical and strategic ramifications. By highlighting the deep ties between American corporations and defence contracts, we can better understand the underlying forces shaping America's war policies and serving big business rather than the people.

Geopolitical manoeuvring: when allies become strategic assets

In the context of international relations, geopolitical manoeuvring often involves the strategic alignment of nations to serve their mutual interests. However, the dynamics of such manoeuvring are complex and multifaceted, often intertwining economic, military, and geopolitical considerations. After the Second World War, the United States found itself in a position of unprecedented global influence. It sought to consolidate its power and contain the spread of communism. As part of this strategy, the United States identified certain allies as crucial strategic assets in different regions based on their geostrategic importance and their potential to counter perceived threats. These alliances were not based solely on ideological affinity or shared values, but rather on pragmatic calculations of power and influence.

The economic dimension played a central role in this process. Indeed, these alliances often involved trade agreements, arms sales and the exploitation of resources that served the economic interests of both parties. Furthermore, providing military aid and transferring technology to allied nations strengthened these relationships, amplifying their strategic importance. The intertwining of economic and geopolitical interests gave rise to complex networks of influence where financial incentives and strategic objectives became inextricably linked.

Through carefully orchestrated diplomatic efforts and behind-the-scenes negotiations, the United States cultivated and exploited these alliances to advance its broader geopolitical agenda, often at the expense of democratic principles or the sovereignty of other nations. This has created a network of dependencies in which allies are not just partners but pawns in a larger geopolitical game.

These considerations emphasise how the pursuit of national interests, often driven by economic imperatives, can influence the geopolitical landscape and redefine the concept of strategic alliances. Understanding these complex dynamics is essential to comprehending contemporary world politics, as they demonstrate the ongoing impact of economic and geopolitical factors on international relations.

Narrative construction: How the media shaped American perceptions of fascism

During the rise of fascism, the media played a decisive role in shaping public opinion. At the beginning of the Second World War, for example, fascist regimes were portrayed as a serious threat to democracy and global stability. The rapid dissemination of information transformed public opinion and fostered the formation of a united front against these ideologies. However, examining the economic foundations of the media during this period reveals the complex interplay of power, money, and geopolitical interests.

Corporate ownership and advertising revenue exerted a significant influence over editorial content and narrative framing. As war propaganda gained traction, the alignment of media narratives with government agendas highlighted the convergence of economic and political motivations. This intersection actively shaped and reinforced American perceptions of fascism, often overshadowing nuanced analyses of the actual geopolitical landscape. To analyse historical events and their lasting impact, it is essential to understand the complex relationship between media, money, and politics. Examining the nuances of media influence during anti-fascist movements sheds light on the manipulation of public opinion and provides valuable insights into current political dynamics.

From sensationalist headlines to strategic omissions, the media's portrayal of fascism has had a profound influence on public opinion and political decisions. As policymakers navigated alliances and conflicts, media narratives could dictate public support and influence the trajectory of foreign affairs. These considerations emphasise the enduring legacy of media framing and its correlation with economic and geopolitical forces in the development of national policy. Recognising the multifaceted nature of media narratives enables us to better comprehend the deep-rooted connections between economic incentives, power dynamics, and policy formulation. By critically evaluating the historical role of the media in shaping American perceptions of fascism, we gain indispensable insights into the complex influences at play in contemporary policymaking.

Cold War Transition: Redefining Enemies and Interests

As the world emerged from the devastation of the Second World War, a new era characterised by ideological confrontations and global power struggles began. The Cold War was characterised by a complex interplay of political, economic and strategic interests, with the United States and the Soviet Union seeking to establish dominance on the international stage. This period of transition was characterised by a significant redefinition of enemies and interests in American foreign policy and world affairs.

The Cold War's dynamics were shaped by deeply rooted geopolitical concerns and strategic calculations, influenced by economic imperatives and the ever-present spectre of nuclear annihilation. The emergence of the Soviet Union as a formidable adversary led to a fundamental reappraisal of political alliances and global security architecture, resulting in a new framework of international relations centred on containing communist expansion. This shift in focus led to the formation of alliances with countries perceived as bulwarks against Soviet influence, facilitating the realignment of global power dynamics.

Amid these geopolitical upheavals, the role of money and economic considerations became increasingly important. Defence spending, arms proliferation, and military aid programmes played a crucial role in shaping US foreign policy, driven by the need to maintain strategic leverage and secure economic interests. Lobbyists and special interest groups exerted considerable influence by advocating policies that aligned with their economic agendas, further intertwining monetary interests and geopolitical strategies. The introduction of economic imperatives into global politics blurred moral boundaries, favouring strategic opportunism over ethical considerations.

Thus, the transition from the Cold War was characterised by the convergence of economic, political, and strategic interests, redefining the contours of American foreign policy and highlighting the complexity of power dynamics in international relations. This period of rebalancing paved the way for a prolonged geopolitical stalemate characterised by a delicate balance of power, covert operations, and the constant renegotiation of strategic and economic priorities. Understanding the complexities of this pivotal era sheds light on the enduring impact of the interplay between economic and geopolitical interests on policy formulation and execution, revealing the intricate connections between money, power, and global influence.

The complex role of money: lobbyists, donations and political loyalty

In the complex landscape of policymaking, the role of money cannot be underestimated. Lobbyists and their financial influence hold considerable sway over the development of political agendas, with donations serving as a means to gain access and favourable decisions. As economic and geopolitical interests become increasingly intertwined, the relationship between money and politics becomes a complex network of influence permeating the corridors of power.

Behind every policy lies a network of lobbyists who are strategically deployed to advocate particular agendas. Representing corporations, interest groups or foreign entities, these stakeholders leverage their financial resources to gain access to the political sphere, where monumental decisions are made that affect global affairs. The allure of financial incentives can blur the distinction between national interests and corporate profits, resulting in policies that prioritise economic gains over broader ethical considerations. Furthermore, donations are not merely financial transactions; they foster a culture of political loyalty and reciprocity. When large sums of money are poured into election campaign coffers or organisational funds, an implicit agreement is established that incentivises policymakers to take their donors' concerns into account. This intertwining of financial support and decision-making creates a system in which allegiance to donors becomes entwined with policymaking, diverting attention away from the broader public interest.

From an economic perspective, the links between financial incentives and political decisions are deeply rooted in the pursuit of national prosperity. However, this pursuit can often conflict with ethical imperatives, resulting in decisions favouring short-term gains over long-term consequences. Geopolitically, financial interests influence alignment with foreign powers, steering the course of alliances and partnerships based on economic advantages rather than shared values or principles.

As we explore this complex issue further, it becomes evident that the intersection of money, lobbyists, and donations exerts a significant influence on the trajectory of political discourse and policymaking. While financial support is vital for maintaining democratic processes, the overall impact of monetary influence raises important questions about decision-making integrity and the protection of national interests. Understanding the complexity of these dynamics highlights the urgent need to balance financial influence with the fundamental values that underpin our political systems.

Erosion of principles: economic justifications for modern alliances

Throughout history, the interaction between money and politics has often been central to the formation and maintenance of alliances. In the modern geopolitical landscape, economic interests increasingly permeate the logic underlying international partnerships and cooperation. This evolution has led to a gradual erosion of the moral principles that once guided the formation of alliances. Economic justifications now often overshadow the traditional emphasis on shared values, mutual security and collective prosperity.

The rise of economic realism has influenced the strategic decisions of nations, promoting a more pragmatic approach to forming and maintaining alliances. The pursuit of economic benefits and market access has become a key factor in the decision-making processes of policymakers, often rendering ethical considerations and historical ties secondary. This shift towards self-interest has obscured the noble goals that historically underpinned alliances, making it more difficult to establish lasting and genuine cooperative relationships. Furthermore, the intertwining of economic and geopolitical interests has created a complex web of dependencies that exerts significant influence over policy formulation. Nations are compelled to prioritise economic gains for strategic reasons, which makes them vulnerable to subtle coercion from more powerful economic actors.

As multinational corporations and financial institutions assert their influence, the boundaries between diplomacy, commerce and power projection are becoming increasingly blurred, thereby complicating the traditional narrative of interstate relations. In this context, ideological alignments and historical alliances often take a back seat to the demands of trade agreements, investment opportunities and resource acquisition. The allure of economic benefits has overshadowed the ideological affinities of the past, resulting in opportunistic partnerships that lack the resilience and integrity that are characteristic of principled associations. Consequently, the moral compass that historically guided international engagements has been eclipsed by the seductive promises of economic prosperity, exposing the fragility of contemporary alliances.

We must recognise the underlying complexities that fuel this erosion of principles. Understanding the intricate dynamics that underpin the economic justification of modern alliances is essential for grasping the motivations and behaviours of nations in the contemporary international arena.

Lessons from history: evaluating policies through a geopolitical lens

When we examine the annals of history, it becomes evident that evaluating policies through a geopolitical lens is crucial for comprehending the intricate web of international relations and power dynamics. Geopolitical factors have often played a central role in shaping government decisions, exerting an influence that transcends mere economic considerations. The interaction between different nations, their strategic interests, and the distribution of resources has always underpinned geopolitical decision-making.

Throughout history, countries have sought to forge alliances and partnerships that align with their long-term geopolitical objectives. These alliances and collaborations are not solely based on economic ties, but are also deeply rooted in broader strategic imperatives. Historically, the quest for territorial dominance, access to vital resources and control over perceived threats has prompted states to form complex networks of geopolitical entanglements.

The intertwining of economic interests and geopolitical strategy often leads to policies prioritising national advantage over ethics. Nations frequently justify their actions by presenting them as essential to their geopolitical security or economic prosperity.

This convergence of economic and geopolitical interests has, in many cases, resulted in ethical standards and human rights being compromised, raising pertinent questions about the moral compass that guides political decisions. Furthermore, the complex interplay of power and influence on the world stage has seen lobbying and financial clout become important determinants of policy formulation.

Backed by substantial financial resources, lobbyists have considerable influence over policy decisions, often steering them towards outcomes that serve particular interests. The links between finance, industry and political power often have a disproportionate impact on geopolitical alignments and political trajectories. Evaluating historical precedents through a geopolitical lens provides valuable insight into the enduring impact of economic and geopolitical interests on policy formulation. This compels us to closely examine the complex web of international relations and unravel the deep motivations that drive nations to prioritise strategic gains over ethical or humanitarian considerations. As we navigate the complexities of contemporary geopolitics, these historical insights are essential for making informed policy decisions based on a deep understanding of the multifaceted forces shaping world affairs.

Charting a New Course: Reflections on Integrity and Future Policy Directions

Examining the geopolitical landscape through the lens of history reveals that money and deep-rooted economic interests have played a central role in shaping American policy. However, amid this reality, there is an opportunity to move towards a path centred on integrity and sustainable foreign policy. To achieve this, it is crucial to critically evaluate past decisions and their underlying motivations. This requires acknowledging the intricate web of economic and geopolitical factors that have traditionally informed policy decisions, frequently at the expense of moral and ethical considerations.

There is an urgent need to reassess the link between financial influences and policymaking. The interaction between corporations, defence contractors, lobbyists and political representatives must be examined closely to mitigate any undue influence. This requires advocating for greater transparency in campaign financing, lobbying activities and interactions between corporations and governments, to preserve the integrity of decision-making processes. Furthermore, when considering future policy directions, the well-being of global populations must be prioritised over limited economic gains.

Rethinking diplomacy and international relations from a

humanitarian perspective can help us work towards a more equitable and just world order. This requires realigning strategic alliances based on shared values and mutual respect rather than short-term economic or military advantages.

Promoting ethical leadership in political spheres is also vital to ensure that political discussions are conducted with integrity. Leaders must be guided not only by the lure of economic prosperity but also by their moral obligation to defend human rights, foster peace, and promote social justice on a global scale. Policies aimed at resolving conflicts, reducing poverty and ensuring sustainable development must be prioritised over short-term economic achievements.

In conclusion, as we reflect on past mistakes influenced by monetary and geopolitical interests, a change of course is imperative. By adopting a diplomatic approach based on integrity and empathy, the United States can develop policies that respect human dignity and promote collective progress.

However, with talk of a post-American world already underway, the big question remains: can the American system be reformed, or is it too late?

Recommended Reading

Theoretical framework

Karoui, Hichem, La sociologie des relations internationales: pouvoir, culture et changement. GEW. London. 2025.

— The Sociology of International Relations: Power, Culture and Change. Global East-West, London, 2025.

— Navigating Uncertainty: The Future of Global Governance and Influence. Global East-West 2024.

— Power Revolving Doors: The Shaping of American Perception of Middle East Studies. A Middle East Studies Book. (Charleston, S.C. USA. 2013.)

— L'administration Bush au Moyen-Orient. (French). Middle East Books (Paris: 2013).

— The Bush II Years in the Middle East (2000-2008) A case study in the sociology of international relations. Middle East Books (Paris - South Carolina: 2012).

General frameworks relating to power and democracy in the United States

Gilpin, Robert. *The Political Economy of International Relations.* Princeton, NJ: Princeton University Press, 1987.

Blum, William. *Killing Hope: U.S. Military and CIA Interventions since World War II.* London: Zed Books, 2003.

Chomsky, Noam, and Edward S. Herman. *Manufacturing Consent: The Political Economy of the Mass Media.* New York: Pantheon Books, 1988.

Mearsheimer, John J. *The Tragedy of Great Power Politics.* Updated ed. New York: W. W. Norton, 2014.

On lobbying, election campaign financing and American foreign policy

Baumgartner, Frank R., and Beth L. Leech. *Basic Interests: The Importance of Groups in Politics and in Political Science.* Princeton, NJ: Princeton University Press, 1998.

Berry, Jeffrey M., and Clyde Wilcox. *The Interest Group Society.* 6th ed. New York: Routledge, 2018.

Drutman, Lee. *The Business of America Is Lobbying: How Corporations Became Politicized and Politics Became More Corporate.* New York: Oxford University Press, 2015.

Ferguson, Charles H. *Lobbyists: The Reawakening of American Influence.* New York: Vintage Books, 2008. (Relevant to Chapter 7 and the general theme of lobbying influencing policy.)

Hacker, Jacob S., and Paul Pierson. *American Politics*

in an Age of Inequality. Cambridge, MA: Harvard University Press, 2020. (Relevant to Chapter 1 on the influence of wealth on the political structure and the erosion of democratic principles.)

Lessig, Lawrence. Republic, Lost: How Money Corrupts Congress—and a Plan to Stop It. New York: Twelve, 2011.

Merton, Robert K. Social Theory and Social Structure. Revised and enlarged ed. New York: The Free Press, 1968. (While broader, concepts of entrenched interests and bureaucracy might inform the discussion on the military-industrial complex (Chapter 3).)

Schattschneider, E. E. The Semisovereign People: A Realist's View of Democracy in America. New York: Holt, Rinehart and Winston, 1960. (A classic text on how organized interests dominate the political process, highly relevant to the book's central thesis.)

American foreign policy, geopolitics and the Cold War

Gaddis, John Lewis. Strategies of Containment: A Critical Appraisal of Postwar American National Security Policy. New York: Oxford University Press, 2005. (Relevant to Chapters 2, 3, and 5 concerning the Cold War, containment policy (Truman Doctrine), and the structure of the post-war order.)

Harvey, David. The New Imperialism. Oxford: Oxford University Press, 2003. (Relevant to Chapter 12 and the critique of "anti-popular wars" and the overall theme of economic expansionism and imperialism.)

Kolko, Gabriel. *The Politics of War: The World and United States Foreign Policy, 1941–1945*. New York: Pantheon Books, 1990. (Relevant to Chapter 2 on the economic motivations behind US involvement in WWII and post-war planning.)

Leffler, Melvyn P. *For the Soul of Mankind: The United States and the Cold War*. New York: Hill and Wang, 2007. (Provides context for the ideological and geopolitical framework discussed in Chapter 5.)

On American foreign policy, imperialism and hegemony

Bacevich, Andrew J. *The New American Militarism: How Americans Are Seduced by War*. New York: Oxford University Press, 2013.

Johnson, Chalmers. *The Sorrows of Empire: Militarism, Secrecy, and the End of the Republic*. New York: Metropolitan Books, 2004.

Grandin, Greg. *Empire's Workshop: Latin America, the United States, and the Making of an Imperial Republic*. New York: Metropolitan Books, 2006.

Nye, Joseph S. *The Future of Power*. New York: PublicAffairs, 2011.

Pease, Donald E. *The New American Exceptionalism*. Minneapolis: University of Minnesota Press, 2009.

On relations between the United States and Israel, the Middle East and the occupation

Avnery, Uri. *My Friend the Enemy.* London: Lawrence Hill Books, 1986. (Offers a historical and critical perspective on the region, useful context for Chapter 5.)

Finkelstein, Norman G. *Image and Reality of the Israel-Palestine Conflict.* 2nd ed. London: Verso, 2003. (Highly relevant to Chapters 4, 9, and 11, as Finkelstein frequently analyzes the role of lobbying and US policy in shaping the narrative and supporting Israeli actions.)

Said, Edward W. *The Question of Palestine.* New York: Vintage Books, 1980. (Essential background for understanding the critique of colonial dynamics and the marginalization of Palestinian rights, referenced in Chapters 4, 9, and 11.)

Tibi, Bassam. *The Crisis of Modern Islam: Hand in Hand with the West.* Reading: Ithaca Press, 1988. (Provides context for the rise of Arab nationalism and the geopolitical context discussed in Chapter 5.)

About the 'Israeli lobby' and American foreign policy

Mearsheimer, John J., and Stephen M. Walt. *The Israel Lobby and U.S. Foreign Policy.* New York: Farrar, Straus and Giroux, 2007.

Finkelstein, Norman G. *Old Wine, Broken Bottle: Ari Shavit's Promised Land.* London: Verso, 2014.

Thrall, Nathan. *The Only Language They Understand:*

Forcing Compromise in Israel and Palestine. New York: Metropolitan Books, 2017.

Beattie, Kirk J. Congress and the Shaping of the Middle East. Gainesville: University Press of Florida, 2016.

Judis, John B. Genesis: Truman, American Jews, and the Origins of the Arab/Israeli Conflict. New York: Farrar, Straus and Giroux, 2014.

Money, media influence and control of discourse

Herman, Edward S., and Noam Chomsky. *Manufacturing Consent: The Political Economy of the Mass Media.* New York: Pantheon Books, 1988. (A foundational text on how media structures align with state and corporate interests, directly applicable to Chapter 8.)

McChesney, Robert W. *The Problem of the Media: U.S. Communication Politics in the 21st Century.* New York: Monthly Review Press, 2004. (Addresses modern media ownership, financing, and the resulting influence on public discourse, relevant to Chapter 8.)

Dean, Jodie. *Publicity's Secret: How Technoculture Capitalizes on Democracy.* Ithaca, NY: Cornell University Press, 2002.

Parenti, Michael. *Inventing Reality: The Politics of News Media.* 2nd ed. New York: St. Martin's Press, 1993.

McChesney, Robert W. *Rich Media, Poor Democracy: Communication Politics in Dubious Times.* New York: The New Press, 1999.

Nichols, John, and Robert W. McChesney. *Dollarocracy: How the Money and Media Election Complex Is Destroying*

America. New York: Nation Books, 2013.

Scientific and policy documents available online (open access)

American Society of International Law. "United States Practice Regarding the International Criminal Court." ASIL Insights 27 (no. 4, 2023), https://www.asil.org.

Pew Research Center. "U.S. Image Abroad Rebounds with Transition from Trump to Biden, but Many Raise Concerns about American Democracy." June 2021. https://www.pewresearch.org.

Transparency International. *Lobbying in the European Union and the United States: A Comparative Overview*. Berlin: Transparency International, 2015. https://www.transparency.org.

United Nations Human Rights Council. *Report of the Special Rapporteur on the Situation of Human Rights in the Palestinian Territories Occupied since 1967*. Geneva: UNOHCHR, 2024. https://www.ohchr.org.

www.ingramcontent.com/pod-product-compliance
Lightning Source LLC
Chambersburg PA
CBHW031150020426
42333CB00013B/588